The Good Coach

Pages from the Playbook of Jesus

by Scott Smith

Published by Better Together Publishing

Raleigh NC

USA

The publisher does not have any control over and does not assume any responsibility for author(s) or third party websites or their content.

ISBN-13: 978-0692135976 (Better Together Publishing)

ISBN-10: 0692135979

Cover Design by Janel Springer

Table of Contents

Introduction 1

Part 1: A Biblical Perspective on Coaching 7
   Chapter 1: A Tough Season.......................................7
   Chapter 2: Getting the Right View 19
   Chapter 3: Perspective on Ourselves........................25
   Chapter 4: The Highest Calling.................................31
   Chapter 5: Misplaced Passion 47
   Chapter 6: Work as an Offering 55
   Chapter 7: Balancing Career and Family 59

Part 2: Leadership Principles from the Master Coach.........67
   Chapter 8: The Teacher, the Training, and the Task 69
   Chapter 9: The Unseen 79
   Chapter 10: The 11th-Hour Principle 89
   Chapter 11: Principles of Preparation.......................97
   Chapter 12: The Power of a Coach's Words 107
   Chapter 13: Adversity Is an Asset 113
   Chapter 14: Winning the Hearts of Your Athletes 119
   Chapter 15: Team Unity 125

Introduction

I have been on a twenty-eight-year journey called coaching, and the writing of this book has been a big part of it. Eight years ago, when I began to write down a few ideas in my journal, the Lord stirred something in my heart. I started to understand that the ideas and perspective I received from Him could add value to other coaches' lives. The closer I began to examine the life of Christ, the more I discovered the practical wisdom in the leadership principles He used. The parallels between my journey as a coach and the ministry and life of Jesus became apparent to me. Surely, the perspective and principles of the Good Coach were needed in the coaching profession. As the Lord revealed these things to me, I began to see how I have woefully fallen short as a leader and a coach. It is a constant struggle to have the right perspective on my job, the people I lead, and the challenges we face in our profession.

Every page from the playbook of Jesus is full of wisdom from the greatest leader and coach to ever live. I realize that Christ provides the model for any profession, not just coaching, but I feel a special connection to Him when I read Hebrews 4:15: "For we do not have a high priest who is unable to empathize with our weaknesses, but we have one who has been tempted in every way, just as we are—yet he did not sin." He has stood where I am standing now. In terms of leading people and taking them somewhere they can't go by themselves, Jesus can empathize with me. That's refreshing and encouraging.

My career as a coach has a lot of parallels with my faith journey. I am discovering that the journey is less about me accomplishing something and more about me becoming something. God's promise I hang my hat on is that He is accomplishing something *in* me, not *for* me. It would be nice to be able to say that following the Good Coach's advice will guarantee you a winning season or championship. It just doesn't work that way. God doesn't have the heart for championships. He has a heart for people.

Coaches can get so caught up in what is important now that we forget what is most important. The things that consume our time and energy now are indeed vital. In some cases, our very jobs and livelihoods depend on them. But if we are not careful, we can neglect what is most important—our relationship with God. Where are you in your journey? Are you in a position that you can lead your family and the athletes He has entrusted to you? In the book *3D Coach*, author Jeff Duke writes, "You can't be a tour guide to a place you have never been." He is referring to the third dimension of coaching that challenges us to a deeper relationship with God. It is from this third dimension that we can coach and lead most effectively.

Coaching is an honorable and admirable profession. Some of the best men and women I have ever known are coaches. Hardworking, trustworthy people with professional and personal integrity fill the coaching profession at all levels from peewee to the pros. My relationships with these coaches have made me a better person, and I am proud that I have chosen this profession.

Like many of you, I enjoy talking with other coaches about the X's and O's of our game, the latest coaching techniques, and game strategies. I find learning from others very productive, and I am always looking for new ideas and better ways of doing things. It has been said that the most significant compliment we can pay our fellow coaches is to copy their success or steal a page out of their playbook. One coach has taught me more than anyone else, and I want to introduce you to Him. His name is Coach Jesus, and He would love to share His methods with you. You know Him as a Carpenter, Healer, Miracle Worker, and hopefully as your Savior. If you take a closer look, however, you will see that He was a coach. As a matter of fact, I can't think of any other profession His life and ministry were more like.

Just as you would seek advice from a wise coach, why not sit down with Jesus and find out how He coached His team? A simple verse in the Gospel of Matthew outlines Christ's mission on earth and sounds a lot like the job description of a coach. His challenge to His disciples is this: "Follow Me, and I will make you fishers of men" (Matt. 4:19, NASB). In this short verse, Jesus's words included three important challenges: First, He asks His disciples to commit to a teacher, a training process, and a task. Isn't this essentially what coaches do today? Aren't we asking the same of our athletes? We want them to trust our leadership and follow us first. Second, we want them to commit themselves to a process of training. Third, we ask them to commit to a task that is bigger than them. Jesus has stood in our shoes. He knows the challenge of trying to get individuals to put aside personal goals in order to accomplish the goals of the team. Fishing for men was not high on His disciples' list of priorities, but they bought into the challenge and turned the world upside down. Jesus took a handful of men from all walks of life and molded them into a team.

His team consisted of tax collectors and fishermen; these guys would not be considered five-star athletes by any means. Like us, He had to lead, teach, train, and motivate them. What a coaching job! Christ should have received the Coach of the Year award for what His team accomplished. We can learn a lot from the way He handled His players and His critics, and how He accomplished what He was sent to do.

This book consists of two parts. Part I includes a biblical perspective on issues coaches face. *Perspective* is simply the way we look at things or the starting point that is crucial to how we think and how we act. Perspective is not a philosophy or coaching advice, but simply a lens we look through. I pray that the ideas in this section will challenge the way you view yourself, your players, and your careers.

Part II includes leadership principles from Jesus's ministry. These principles are beautiful nuggets of truth found in God's word. I like to call them *timeless truths* because they work today just as they did two thousand years ago. Simple to understand but sometimes hard to follow, these truths are meant to meet coaches right where we are—in the trenches of our jobs. I pray this section will challenge you to copy pages from the playbook of Jesus.

At the end of each chapter, there will be a few questions to help you reflect on what you have read in each section. Take a minute and jot down your thoughts to solidify the concepts as well as give you actionable ways to use them in your life.

Part 1

God whispers to us in our pleasures, speaks in our consciences,
but shouts in our pains. It is his megaphone to rouse a deaf world.

—C. S. Lewis

1
A Tough Season

Coaches' lives are divided and dictated by seasons. Off-season, preseason, in-season, and postseason activities continue in exact cycles year after year. I have discovered that life is a lot like that. Single life, married life, married with kids, parenting teens, and the empty nest are seasons we find ourselves in. Then there are seasons of discontentment, silence from God, waiting, confusion, fear, pain, and brokenness. These seasons can be very long; at least, it seems that way when we are going through them.

Unlike the seasons that can be measured by wins and losses, these seasons don't have a clear-cut ending. When you find yourself in one of these stormy seasons, life can be tough. But I believe God uses seasons and storms in our lives to accomplish His work in us.

7

In fact, I believe we should continue to praise him through the storm, just like the popular song "Praise You in This Storm" by Casting Crowns talks about. To be honest though, in the past, I disliked this song because of the one line that describes God as the God who gives and takes away. It was the part about God taking away that I did not like. It bothered me that God would take something away from me, and I found it difficult to be able to praise Him under those circumstances. In 2011, I came to understand what it meant to praise God in the storm.

In order for you to appreciate this story fully, I must first rewind several years. The story actually starts with my wife several years before we met. Wendy was widowed at a young age. Her husband died in a tragic boating accident while she was pregnant with their third child. When I met Wendy some time later, I didn't see a widow with three toddlers. I saw a woman in love with God, who had learned to live above her circumstances; that really attracted me to her. In coaching terms, you might say that she had learned to play while hurt, and she was not watching from the sidelines. She had a peace and joy about her that made her a very beautiful person. She had weathered her storm and had come out on the other end a Godly woman. She could have chosen to become bitter, but instead, she clung to God in this challenging season, showing great strength and faith. It is this same strength that would be my inspiration during the storm Wendy and I faced together many years later.

Shortly after meeting, we started dating, and a year and eight months later we got married on December 16, 1995. Incidentally, the date was strategically positioned in between football and wrestling seasons—the two sports I coached. From the beginning, my wife was very understanding about the demands of coaching. As a matter of fact, the wedding date was on the same date as the Georgia High School State Football Championship. Poor planning on our part. That particular season, we had an outstanding team, and as we entered the playoffs, it looked feasible that we might be playing on December 16, our wedding date. The plan was to get married early in the day, then attend the football game if the team advanced to the final game. Well, we lost out in the quarter-finals, so it never became an issue. I guess it was the Lord's way of getting my priorities in order. Not really, I still get upset when I think of losing that game.

So, getting back to the story, I went from being single and never married to a husband and instant father of three. I sort of skipped the season of married with no children. I soon adopted Nikki, Zack, and Jamie, who were ages three, four, and five. All three of the kids quickly embraced me as their father. My family also welcomed the kids and Wendy, and for that, I am profoundly grateful. Chase came along in 1998. Now we were six.

Storms started to brew during the teen years. It was a season of life that was very challenging for Wendy and me. Our biggest concern was for Zack. As a youngster and in his early teens, he was very devoted to the Lord. Somewhere along the way though, Satan and his lies crept into Zack's mind. He became a prodigal in his faith, questioning God and rebelling against our authority. We prayed, sought counsel, showed tough love, and did all we knew to do. We gave it all to the Lord, hoping that this tumultuous season would end. This season of our life seemed to drag on forever. One line in the song "Praise You in this Storm" really rang true to us:

> *I was sure by now, God you would have reached down*
> *And wiped our tears away,*
> *Stepped in and saved the day.*
> *But once again, I say amen*
> *That it's still raining*

Oh, how we prayed and hoped God would step in! We knew it was only God who could bring Zack back. We cried out to God for help, but Zack's heart remained callous to God. Then the attacks on us came: What had we done wrong? Maybe we should have done things differently. Perhaps we didn't show Zack enough love, or this wouldn't be happening. Fortunately, we were surrounded by godly people who were able to help us expose these lies of the devil. But it still was a tough season. The storm just seemed to persist. Instead of subsiding, the storm intensified.

On September of 2011, Zack tragically took his own life. He was twenty. We will never fully understand why, and we will always have a part of us that is missing. Fortunately, the bridge was not burned in my relationship with Zack. We got a visit from him two weeks before his death, and I hugged him and told him I loved him.

Zack had joined the navy, and I think he was beginning to mature. My brother-in-law, Joe, had a conversation with him a few months before his death. He opened up to Joe and told him he appreciated me and recognized that his behavior had been harmful to our family. I have always believed that the ability to confess your wrongs to someone else is a sign of maturity. I am certain that Zack was beginning to give in to the Spirit of God working in his life. He had recently had some storms in his personal and professional life, and I know the Lord was nudging at his heart.

Although Zack's life was short and filled with turmoil toward the end, he did bring us much joy. He was a child of God and a beautiful creation made in His image. He was a loving, loyal, creative, quick-witted, intelligent, and compassionate person. His heart was big; showing love and loyalty came easily to him. He quickly embraced me as his father and regularly displayed love and loyalty to his family and friends. His God-given sense of protection and loyalty made him an outstanding military serviceman. When he put his mind to doing something, he was very determined and worked hard to reach his goals. He worked many hours to achieve the rank of Eagle Scout. He was also one of the hardest workers on my wrestling team. I was proud of him as a father and a coach. When his friend Jake was diagnosed with cancer, he unselfishly served him and was right by his side through the surgeries and treatments. I will always remember these qualities about Zack. Certainly, I still experience the pain of losing him, but when I choose to remember him in this way, I experience joy. I choose to remember him in this way because this is how he was created. Like all of us, he was an image bearer of the God of the universe. When you look upon the image of God, it brings you joy, not pain.

I know that the Lord never let go of Zack. I am sure of this because I believe in amazing grace. I am thankful that God is the dispenser of grace, not me. You see, I looked at Zack's rebellion and callousness and saw a kid who had turned his back on God. God doesn't see that. His grace is too big and amazing. His grace does not allow him to see Zack through the same eyes that I did. I tend to place a lot of emphasis on what people deserve. Maybe all coaches are like that to a degree. We preach to our athletes that they must work hard so they will be deserving of victories. But God doesn't dispense things to us based on merit. He dispenses gifts, not wages. After Zack's death, I was drawn to the concept of grace. I read *What's So Amazing about Grace?* by Phillip Yancey. This book really ministered to me. He writes: "In the bottom line realm of ungrace, some deserve more than others, in the realm of grace, the word deserve does not even apply."

We live in a world filled with ungrace. There is little room for error. We see it magnified in our profession. Players and coaches who don't perform are quickly replaced. It is refreshing to take a long look at the amazing grace of God. I found great comfort in God's grace after Zack's death. I continue to find peace and comfort when I think of God's amazing grace.

Things were a blur in the days following Zack's death. I can't even begin to thank all the people who reached out to us. We were truly blessed. Our home was filled with family and friends who grieved with us and loved us through this difficult time. We witnessed the body of Christ at work in our lives, and it was very comforting. It felt like the arms of Jesus Himself were wrapping around us. God was stepping in and wiping our tears away. We experienced God as a healer. Our pain was met by the Great Healer, and I believe Zack's was too.

All this took place right in the middle of a football season. I missed two games and a week of practice. While I was away from the team, the coaches and players reached out to us, and that meant a lot. I received encouraging texts from players assuring me of their prayers and that they would rally and play in support of my family and me. The night after Zack's death, Wendy, my son Chase, and I, listened to our game on the radio. We were all emotionally spent, but somehow we needed to be a part of the game that night. Listening to the game made things feel normal. Winning had also become the norm during our football seasons. The team was on a thirty-four game winning streak including two consecutive state championships. But this night, things were different. I wasn't there, and it felt strange, even under our circumstances. It appeared the team was also playing like something wasn't right. Even the radio announcers were making comments about the team's unusual lackluster performance. We were not playing on all cylinders. We were on the road and down late in the fourth quarter to an excellent football team. Our defense had played a tremendous game, giving us a chance to win. Our offense, however, was struggling to move the ball, and it appeared that the winning streak would come to an end. Then suddenly, we scored on a short pass that broke for the game-winning touchdown. Back at home, the cheers of joy coming from my bedroom were mixed with tears and hugs.

It is hard to describe the mix of emotions we were feeling, but somehow, I knew our tears represented the beginning of the healing process. This win was big for my family and me. Perhaps even bigger than the two previous state championship games we won. The Lord had used the coaches and players of Sandy Creek High School as His instruments to begin the healing process in our lives. A few days later, dressed in their red jerseys, the team came to Zack's memorial service, and I was able to hug the coaches and players and thank them for what they had done. I will always remember and cherish the love I received from my football family.

In the days following Zack's death, I was also drawn to Tony Dungy's story. Coach Dungy also had a son who took his life. I had already read his book Quiet Strength, and I decided to pick it up again and read the chapter that documents his stormy season. I have always admired Coach Dungy, and I guess I was seeking some counsel and comfort from his words. His story gave me hope that I too could move forward with faith and strength. There were many similarities in our stories, and his testimony reinforced the things I had always believed to be true. The manner in which he dealt with his tragedy challenged me to trust in the goodness of God.

As I previously mentioned, my wife, Wendy, has been my biggest inspiration through this challenging season. I have always believed that the greatest love that can be found on earth is the love a mother has for her child. That means the greatest pain on earth is the pain a mother feels when she loses a child. Wendy's faith has matched her pain. Even in her great pain, she has remained steady in her faith. What a godly example and what a blessing our family has! Her strength, however, is not her own; it comes from the Lord. She has clung to the Lord and has shown our family how to trust God through the storms of life.

My wife and I continue to lean on each other. We can often sense each other's pain even before a word is spoken. We both understand that there will always be a void in our life that can never be replaced, and that time will never completely heal our broken hearts. However, in the midst of our pain, we do find hope and comfort in God's unchanging truths. The cross and the empty tomb tell us that grace wins and that Zack's life was not defined by one decision. It tells us that one day, we will be reunited with Zack. We believe in faith that this reunion will take place. It is not a flimsy hope based on wishful thinking, but a strong belief that is an anchor for our soul, strong and secure.

Another song that has a lot of meaning to me is "Believe" by Brooks & Dunn. I like it because it speaks of a belief that is strong and secure even in the midst of the painful seasons of life. The song tells the story of an old man, Mr. Wrigley, who builds a relationship with a young boy and imparts wisdom to him through casual conversations on an old porch swing. Mr. Wrigley shares his stormy season with the lad. Early in his life, he experienced the loss of his wife and son. When asked about how he deals with this pain, he responds, "I'll see my wife and son in just a little while." There is something about this statement that comforts and encourages me. It is the belief that one day, we will see Zack again, and that day is not that far away. Time on earth is put in perspective when compared to all of eternity. The longer I live, the more I realize that we are here for just a little while and that soon, we will cross over into eternity, where we will be reunited with the ones we love.

In the song, Mr. Wrigley dies several years later, but his influence lives on. The now grown man looks back on his conversations with Mr. Wrigley and realizes the old man taught him much about life. He says, "You know I'm more and more convinced the longer that I live, yeah this can't be, no this can't be, no this can't be all there is." The longer I live, the more I realize and appreciate the truth and perspective in this song. I am discovering that this world has nothing to offer me. There is no position, pleasure, or prize here on earth that can compare or compete with what waits for me in eternity. As the song says, this truth compels me to "raise my hands" in a declaration that I believe, and "bow my head" in humble gratitude for the victory that has already been won through Christ.

Maybe you have had some tough seasons, or perhaps you are in one right now. Or it's a stormy season in your personal life, possibly you haven't seen the win column for a long time, and you fear your job is in jeopardy. It may seem very long, and you don't understand why things are going the way they are. You thought you did all the right things. Shouldn't God have stepped in by now and calmed the storm? I don't know what storms you have faced or may be facing. But I do know God holds your tears. In the midst of my storms, I felt the presence of God holding my family and me. I know He wants to wrap His arms around you and be your healer too.

Questions for reflection

1. Where does the world look to find hope? Why can we look to Jesus for hope in the midst of the storms of life?
2. Do you have people in your life who can surround you and be the arms of Jesus in difficult times?
3. What evidence of God's grace do you see in your life?

2
Getting the Right View

One of my favorite movies is *Evan Almighty*. It is a great family-friendly movie with some powerful messages. The plot of the story is that God, played by Morgan Freeman, has chosen Evan Baxter, played by Steve Carell, to build a modern-day ark. When Evan responds to God that building an ark is really not part of his plans, God laughs. It's a classic movie scene that sheds light on the important truth that God's plans for our lives don't always match ours. Coaches are very strategic and careful when it comes to making plans. Sometimes, offensive coordinators even script out the first ten plays of a ball game. Planning involves anticipation, expectation, and most importantly, hope. At the beginning of our seasons, hopes are high as the plan is put into action. The reality of our profession, however, is that, sometimes, things don't go according to plan. What we anticipated happening doesn't happen. Our expectations for teams and ourselves are not met, and the high hopes we had are lost.

So, how do we respond? Our response to things we can't control is crucial, and it is closely tied to a key word: perspective. *Perspective* is the lens through which we view life. Simply put, it is how we look at things. Before we respond, we must have the proper perspective. Many times in my career, I have reacted to things without first getting God's perspective. When this happens, the outcome is usually not good. Like Evan Baxter (Noah), I've got plans, and when events occur that disrupt my plans, I tend to respond in inappropriate and ungodly ways. If we could only see things through the lens God sees them. If we could briefly get God's perspective, we would view things a lot differently and respond to them appropriately. I am not suggesting that we never get upset and that we allow everything to roll off our back without any emotion. Passion and emotion are God-given qualities that we need to be successful. What we desperately need, though, is God's perspective. Sometimes, God doesn't reveal His entire plan to us, but He will show us His perspective. With His perspective, we will begin to view our athletes, our careers, and ourselves as He does.

In Psalm 73, we read about how we can get the right perspective. The psalmist starts the chapter by proclaiming the goodness of God, but his journey in discovering this truth was a bit of a roller coaster. He admits that his feet "had almost slipped" and he had "nearly lost his foothold."

This instability was due to a warped perspective on the events in his life. He is troubled by the ways of the wicked and the seemingly absent hand of God to do anything about it. Why does God allow the wicked to go unpunished? Why do the wicked seem to have abundance and prosperity? He feels slighted by God, and that his best efforts to live a holy life have been in vain. Then in verse 17, there is an amazing turn in his perspective. He says, "Till I entered the sanctuary of God; then I understood their final destiny." From this point onward, he changes his perspective. The wicked are still present, but the psalmist's heart is completely changed. The rest of the chapter is filled with the truth about the wicked and the truth about himself. Toward the end of the chapter, another shift occurs, from focusing on the wicked to focusing on his relationship with God. He learns the proper perspective on his life, and most importantly, he learns to be content with God regardless of the circumstances around him.

He writes: "Whom have I in heaven but you? And besides you, I desire nothing on earth.

My flesh and my heart may fail. But God is the strength of my heart and my portion forever" (Ps. 73:25-26, NASB).

So, how did he do it? What caused the significant change in perspective? It was his time in the sanctuary. His time in the presence of God made all the difference. There is no substitute for time with God. Nothing changes us like being in His presence. No sermon, no book, or no person can change your perspective like being in the presence of the God of the universe. My life is full of Psalm 73:17 moments. I often respond to events out of frustration because the events that I can't control are just not a part of my plans.

I make plans for my marriage, kids, finances, and career, and when things don't go accordingly, I develop a wrong perspective.

What about you? Has your job given you a warped perspective that leaves you feeling as if God has forgotten about you? The grind of our jobs, losing seasons, unappreciative athletes, fans, and parents all have their way of blurring our vision and making us feel that our hard work is in vain. Maybe it has nothing to do with your job. Could it be that problems at home have consumed you to the point that you feel hopeless? The good news is that there is always hope. God can change your perspective and help you see things as He sees them. It has been said that life is 10 percent circumstances and 90 percent how you respond to your circumstances. Responding properly starts with seeing things correctly—this is our challenge.

The application of this principle is simple: Spend time with God. Read His word. Pray. Schedule time to do these things just like you would schedule a meeting with anyone else. This is the most important thing we can do.

If time with God is the most important thing, then I believe putting yourself in the right environment is a close second. Gaining the right perspective is one thing, but keeping it is another, and I have found this to be one of the biggest challenges in my personal and professional life. It is not really a onetime thing that you arrive at and never have to worry about again. I have found it to be a constant struggle that sometimes leaves me feeling frustrated and defeated. This struggle is, of course, a spiritual battle that takes place first of all in our minds. The enemy works overtime to feed our hearts and minds with lies that keep us from seeing things through heavenly lenses. That is why it is crucial that we have truth spoken into our lives. Are we putting ourselves in the right environments to hear and be exposed to the truth? The Lord uses His Word, His Spirit, and His people to speak truth into our lives.

How I cherish the words of truth that have been spoken into my life. I have received truth from the words of friends and family, from the words of songs, and from the words of countless speakers, teachers, authors, and preachers of God's word. And, of course, I have received truth from the written word of God that the Holy Spirit illuminated in my heart as I opened it and read. My hope in writing this book is that it will speak truth into your life and help you combat the lies of the enemy.

Questions for reflection

1. When God's plans are different than our own, what perspective should we take?
2. Can you identify any faulty perspective you have in your personal or professional life? What would it look like to put yourself in God's presence so you can get His perspective?

3. Do you surround yourself with God's people to help you keep perspective? If not, find a small group or a Bible study to join and be open to God working in your life. You will not regret it.

3
Perspective on Ourselves

The enemy does not want us to see through the lens of truth. He wants to distort and blur our perspective, especially when it comes to how we view ourselves. He will try to chip away at our confidence by getting us to attach our self-worth to our performance. If we fall into this trap, the win-loss column becomes the standard by which we judge ourselves. Of course, this works both ways. Winning gives us confidence and a positive view of ourselves, and losing erodes our confidence and causes us to question who we are and what we are doing. Either way, our view of ourselves is rooted in the wrong thing.

It is the same trap that keeps many people from accepting the grace of Jesus. There is a spiritual win-loss column for many people. Some believe they must perform to win God's favor, or they must clean themselves up before they can come to God. He would never accept me the way I am. They see themselves in the loss column. Others get a sense of self-righteousness by doing certain religious things. The more they do for God, the more wins they accumulate. In the end, if the wins outweigh the losses, God will accept them. Fortunately, there are no win-loss columns in heaven. There is only one victory that matters—the victory of the empty tomb. The song "Arise My Love" by NewSong sums it up perfectly:

> *Sin, where are your shackles?*
> *Death, where is your sting?*
> *Hell has been defeated*
> *The grave could not hold the King*

Christ has already won the victory for us! What a relief to know that we don't have to work our way into the presence of God. Our identity is found in the finished work of the cross.

It is the victory that Jesus won on the cross that gives us validation. That means our walk in public is based on our position in private. The two can't be separated because the Spirit and power of God live in us. When we understand this truth, we are free to be who God created us to be and liberated from being concerned about the opinions of others. Emancipated to live and coach in such a way that serves others and seeks to meet their needs. Free from having to prove our worth through our careers. This freedom allows me to be laser focused on what makes my team and athletes better. Understanding this principle and living by it makes us a better coach.

This is not as easy as it sounds. We are competitive by nature, and winning is important. When things are going well with our teams, we feel much better about life. When the losses begin to stack up, it can be very discouraging. When that happens, we must be able to separate our professional and personal worth. I was fortunate to coach a football team that won three Georgia State Championships in four years.

During that run, we had a forty-one-game winning streak. It was quite a ride. It was an experience for which I am humbled and very grateful that the Lord allowed me to be a part. That experience, however, does not define me as a coach or as a man. It doesn't describe me any more than going 2–8 and 1–9 at my next coaching job. A losing streak shouldn't change how we view ourselves. If it does, then chances are we have the wrong perspective. There was a season in my career when I struggled with seeing myself through the proper lens. I was on a job search year after year to find a bigger and better job, but the Lord was not opening any doors. Essentially, I was looking for others to validate me. If I got called in for an interview, then it made me feel good about myself. If I got turned down for the job, I felt discouraged and it affected my confidence. It was a real struggle. I had a hard time trusting God's plan for my life, and I was not doing a very good job of separating my professional and personal worth. In reality, I was in bondage to my career and the opinions of others. I like to think I have grown to the point of trusting God for my future and not worrying so much about my career path and where that takes me. I like to think I can live by the truth I find in the words of a popular song: "I don't need to see everything just more of you" (We Are Messengers, "Magnify").

For me, "seeing everything" is a control issue. I confess I have control issues, and my wife would agree. I don't like surprises or spontaneous decisions. Maybe this is a good quality for a coach to have, but it can also become a heavy burden that we are not meant to carry. During the 2016 presidential primaries, I was impacted by the concession speech of Marco Rubio. As he was accepting defeat and taking himself out of the race for president, he said this: "We are on the right side, but this year, we are not on the winning side. I am grateful to God in whose hands all things lie. God is perfect. He makes no mistakes. Everything that comes from God is good." Senator Rubio understood that God was sovereign even in the midst of his disappointment and defeat. Analyzing this from a political standpoint would bring you to the conclusion that the voters were the decision makers. They indeed were. But they weren't sovereign. Sovereignty is reserved to God, and we make a mistake when we assume that anyone or anything else holds the reigns in our life. However, it is hard for us to see God's sovereignty and purpose, especially in times of defeat. We just don't have the big picture God sees. We naturally see things from our limited perspective, and when things don't go as planned, it is easy to lose faith. I mean, why would God plant us in a place where we can't win or where we are not appreciated? Why does it seem that our efforts are in vain? Why aren't things working out like we planned or prayed for? It may seem as though we have made a mistake, or maybe God has. But make no mistake—God doesn't make mistakes.

If we are looking at the win-loss column or the trophy shelf as a measuring stick, then we might need to look elsewhere. God has always used people and their circumstances for someone else's benefit. We need to broaden our search to understand God's sovereignty. Think of Joseph, who was sold into slavery only to find himself in a position years later that would save God's people. Think of Esther, who was chosen for "such a time as this." Through her life, the Israelites were once again saved. Joseph and Esther couldn't see this at first, but their faithfulness to God's calling paved the way for God to accomplish something bigger.

I changed jobs a few years ago, and it turned out to be a bad move if you measure it by wins and losses. Professionally speaking, it was a tough situation, and at the time, it was very discouraging. Nothing about that chapter in my life was victorious from a coaching or professional standpoint. Looking back though, I believe the move was really not about me at all. I firmly believe the Lord orchestrated this move for one or two conversations my wife would have with our pastor, Mark Pritchett. The conversations Wendy had with Mark were very instrumental for her to obtain peace and lift a heavy burden she was carrying. Those conversations would not have happened if I had taken another job I was offered the same year.

Many times, this is how God works. Things may seem bad on the surface, but the Lord has a way of using those problematic circumstances for a greater good. In this case, the greater good had nothing to do with me or my career—it was for my wife. I have since changed jobs, but that experience taught me that God doesn't waste a place. In the midst of our transient careers and seasons of defeat, we can still be grateful to God in whose hands all things lie. We can know that God is perfect, that He makes no mistakes, and that everything that comes from God is good.

Questions for reflection

1. What right perspective can we have on winning and losing?
2. Is there a time in your life God used a difficult season or set of circumstances for the greater good? If so, remember what God has done and praise him.
3. How can we avoid the performance trap and remain confident in the midst of defeat?

4
The Highest Calling

As coaches, we are in a position to use our influence and our sport to teach valuable character lessons such as teamwork, unselfish behavior, accountability, a strong work ethic, overcoming adversity, humility, and love for our brothers and sisters. Many coaches institute character education programs that focus on these attributes. The truth is, we need our players to buy into this if our teams are going to reach their full potential. We need high-character people to be the playmakers and leaders on our teams. How many times have you seen teams either rise in the face of great adversity or fold their tents when things got tough? Or maybe you have seen a very talented team with selfish attitudes lose to a less talented team. The rewards of good character are clearly relevant on and off the field.

As Christian coaches, we can't stop at a good character education program. We are sent to the fields of play and into the field of coaching for an even higher calling. Scripture gives coaches a very fitting job description. It tells us we are ambassadors. By definition, ambassadors represent someone else, and never before has there been a greater need to have believers represent God for who He really is. There are so many people whose view of God is

31

distorted, and this breaks God's heart. He longs for those He has created to know Him as a loving Father, and He calls coaches to be His ambassadors. The Lord has a clear message. As His ambassadors, we are to represent Him as a God who is real, relevant, and life-changing. Essentially, He is saying: "I am real, I matter, and I can fulfill you." The amazing thing is that this appeal comes through us.

We are the instruments, the models, and the mouthpieces God uses to get this message out. We must get this message out. Notice the sense of urgency in the scripture: "We are therefore Christ's ambassadors, as though God were making his appeal through us. We implore you on Christ's behalf: Be reconciled to God" (2 Cor. 5:20, NIV). Paul says, "We beg you on behalf of Christ." Clearly, we are the instruments of Christ's appeal, and clearly, this means a lot to God. It is an honor and privilege to be the messengers of such an important appeal. Let us never forget that God's ultimate goal in our coaching is the reconciliation of others to Him. The Lord has given us our jobs for a much higher calling than to win games and championships. He wants us to use our influence and platform to accomplish His purposes. This is our highest calling. I believe coach Bobby Bowden understands this perspective. When asked about his legacy, he said: "I hope the most important thing people say about me is that I accomplished God's purposes in my life." Coach Bowden was one of the most successful coaches in NCAA history, but his legacy of being used by God will far outlive the championships he won. All coaches have a platform. Some are bigger than others. In God's economy, it doesn't matter if you're an assistant who is the low man on the totem pole, or a head coach of a world championship team. You are there for a reason, and God can use you in whatever position you find yourself.

So how do we show our athletes God is real? This is our first task as His ambassadors and perhaps, the most challenging. Many people doubt the existence of God, because their pain is more real than a God they can't see. The disappointments of life are heavy. They have been let down by people. There must not be a God, or if He does exist, He is undoubtedly absent or unconcerned. This is the type of pain athletes carry to our teams. It is often masked and carefully protected. Walls are put up. Egos are inflated to hide the hurt. But deep inside, they are searching for something, something real that can heal their scars and embrace them just like they are. Breaking down these walls can be a challenging task.

Coach Kenneth Miller, who coaches an inner-city football team in Atlanta, knows this challenge firsthand. The majority of his athletes come from single-parent, fatherless homes. They want to be coached up when it comes to football, but they are not interested in spiritual things. They have been hurt and abandoned by the men in their life. Therefore, it is tough for them to open themselves to a God who claims to be a loving Father. I have only observed Coach Miller from a distance, but I have discerned him enough to know that he is a true ambassador for the Lord. He doesn't let the walls his players have built up stop him from representing God as real, relevant, and life-changing. I am inspired by Coach Miller's heart for God and his heart for his players. He understands his highest calling. He isn't just a good football coach who happens to be a Christian. He is an ambassador for the Lord who happens to be a good coach.

If God is real, then He has to be relevant. What good is a God who isn't relevant? Our challenge here is to integrate our faith with our jobs, to show our athletes that God is a part of our careers, that He is in the center of our lives, and that our relationship with Him doesn't stop when we leave church on Sunday. It is one thing for a kid to see their pastor or youth minister live out their faith in practical ways. They are supposed to do that. It is even more powerful when a coach does it. Of course, I don't mean to minimize the importance of the clergy. They too have a tremendous impact on young people. However, a common mistake many Christians make is to put God in a box. I think it's mostly because that's what we have seen modeled for us. We just haven't seen enough lay people living out their faith outside the four walls of a church. Putting God in a box just makes sense because that's all we have really seen. We have our church box where we commune with God through worship, prayer, and the illumination of scripture, but the Lord stays in the box when we are at home or work.

For a coach, one of the greatest challenges is to allow God on the field, in the locker room, and in the coach's office. Where did we get the idea that God doesn't belong in the athletic arena? Do we communicate through omission that faith is irrelevant on the field of play? Do we think it somehow makes us soft or less competitive if we integrate our faith into our work? Do we think or say things like "That church stuff just doesn't work here"? This is a faulty philosophy that prevents God from blessing our lives and our teams and communicates to our athletes that God is not relevant or at least not here, not in sports. If we sow the seeds of irrelevance now, our athletes will learn that He is irrelevant in other areas of their lives down the road—their marriage, career, and parenting. There is a lot more at stake here than meets the eye. We must build into our athletes' hearts and minds that God is relevant to any stage and situation in life. Remember, more is caught than taught. They need to see that we are allowing God to be a part of our coaching.

Finally, our appeal as Christ's ambassadors is to represent him as a life-changing God. Transformation is God's specialty. He transforms broken lives and hearts. He makes all things new; He brings purpose and peace to our lives. He brings us from death to life. His power to change lives can do for us what we can't do for ourselves. Jesus's ministry on earth was all about life change. He taught for transformation, not just information. That sounds a lot like what we do as coaches. We too are in the business of transforming individuals into a team. We ask our athletes to buy in. Buy into our off-season program, our schemes and strategies, our methods, and our team goals. A commitment like this involves sacrifice, hard work, and a denial of self. This type of transformation is a training process. It takes time. Great players and great teams are made, not born. The same can be said for us.

We too must commit to a process of life change. God is still in the business of transformation, and He wants to change us from the inside out. It is a process that we call *sanctification*. It involves us becoming more like Christ and less like us. It means we have to humble ourselves and be coachable. This work is never done. We will never arrive at a point where we can coast. In the coaching profession, we understand this idea. We can't allow our teams to coast on their talent or past accomplishments. If they do, they will get beat.

To illustrate this point, imagine you are dressed in a long white robe. You are in the dark and walking toward a bright light. As you get closer, the light begins to reveal dirty spots on your white robe—large, filthy spots that you can't believe you didn't notice. So, what do you do? You stop and clean it off. Then you continue the walk and notice still more dirty spots. So you stop once again to clean it off. As you draw closer to the light, more dirty spots are revealed. This is how transformation works. This is how we become more like Christ. We deal with the blemishes then we continue our journey.

We walk toward Him (the light), and we listen to His voice along the way. We must allow him to coach us. We can't insist on doing it our way or pouting because He has brought some sin to our attention. We know He loves us and whatever He tells us is in our best interest. To truly represent the life-changing power of God, we have to allow Him to change us.

The Good Coach faced similar challenges with his team. Although Jesus was God in the flesh, He was still an ambassador in the sense that He had to prove the reality of a loving Father to people who doubted. Coach Jesus had the same message we do. His entire ministry revolved around teaching the reality, relevance, and life-changing power of God, and He used His platform to accomplish what God had sent Him to do. It is worth taking a closer look at the life of Jesus because He gives us a model to follow when it comes to coaching our teams.

One of the things we notice about Jesus's coaching style is that He was approachable. His team felt very comfortable coming to Him. Mark 6:30 tells us, "The apostles gathered around Jesus and reported to him all they had done and taught" The apostles felt comfortable approaching Jesus and sharing with Him all the things they had done. In the same way, good coaches are approachable. They know how to relate to the people they lead. There are no walls or restrictions that prevent open and honest dialogue. I'm sure the apostles' report to Jesus revealed their many mistakes and missed opportunities, but Jesus had created an environment in which they felt comfortable sharing with their leader even if it meant sharing their mistakes. This type of open-door policy creates an environment of acceptance and grace. It also allows the leader to get a sense of the heartbeat of the team. More importantly, authenticity and approachability are Christ-like characteristics that young people need to see lived out in their coach. I would even go so far as to say it is essential to show a little vulnerability. I think that is Christ-like too. Seeing Christ in us shows them that our relationship with God is real.

There is something pure about letting others see Jesus through you. It's disarming. It's undeniable. Conversely, there is something uneasy and untrustworthy about a phony. We have to be real. That means there is no pretense, no sham, no posing. What our athletes need to see when they look at us is authenticity. If they sniff out unauthentic behavior, they will quickly write you off. No wonder so many people doubt God's existence when they look around and see Christians trying to be something they are not. Make no mistake— your athletes are looking at you, and you may be the only Jesus they see. It is only through a proper view of Jesus that they can know God is real.

Another quality of Coach Jesus is His clear understanding of His purpose and His focus on accomplishing God's will. It is important to remember that Jesus was a carpenter. That means He had to spend many hours learning His trade. Remember, He was fully man; He didn't automatically know how to build things. We don't read much about the Lord's carpentry skills in scripture, so we have to fill in those blanks with what we know about His nature (the nature of God). We have to assume He was a talented carpenter because He is committed to excellence. No corner cutting. No shabby work. You might even say He was a *master* craftsman. We have to assume He had a strong work ethic and His finished products were always built to the highest standards. His work in crafting wood had many parallels to His work in crafting people.

You start with a raw product, a piece of lumber, and with time, labor, precision, and care, it transforms into something usable and beautiful. I wonder if Jesus ever thought about how His trade paralleled His purpose. As He was working on a piece of furniture, did His mind ever drift to thoughts of how He would soon be transforming people? I think we can be certain that Jesus's work as a carpenter never caused Him to lose sight of His true purpose. His purpose was building people, not patio furniture. Notice the focus and perspective He reveals in the following verses:

"I have come that they may have life, and have it to the full" (John 10:10, NIV), and "The Son of Man did not come to be served, but to serve, and to give his life as a ransom for many" (Mark 10:45, NIV).

Jesus understood that His career as a carpenter was temporary, but His heavenly calling had eternal implications. Therefore, what we read about in the Gospels is the story of how Jesus coached a team, not how He made things with His hands. We see how Coach Jesus led, taught, and motivated His team to turn the world upside down. He was a carpenter by trade, but He lived for a much higher calling. I was once challenged in a sermon to view my profession as a calling and not a career. Callings are from God. Careers can become our god. Callings promise the opportunity to bear fruit and be used by God. Careers promise status, power, and wealth. Callings have eternal significance, and professions have temporary rewards. Coaching, like the carpentry skills of our Lord, is our trade. Our calling, however, is much more than putting a quality product on the field of play. Has building a great program become more about advancing your kingdom than God's?

To coach with proper perspective means that we value people over the program. Decisions are made about what is best for people because we value the individual first. Coach Jesus built a team of disciples that would run through walls for Him. They were totally committed to His cause of becoming fishers of men. Many would eventually die for this cause. How was He able to get such a high commitment level? Most coaches would do anything to get that type of commitment from their players. I believe the answer is simple: He valued people more than a program. He put people first. He was always able to treat people with value while at the same time not compromising the mission of His team. We can do that too. Simon Peter is a great example of Jesus's coaching success. This ordinary fisherman was transformed when Jesus entered His life. He was often brash, impulsive, and prejudiced, and he wavered in his commitment to the Lord, denying Him three times. Jesus could have easily given up on him, but He stayed the course. He continued to make personal investments in this man. These investments paid off in the end.

These investments had eternal significance. By the time Christ was through with him, he was a changed man that would be a key player on Christ's team. Imagine if Jesus had His own agenda and He used His skills as a carpenter to promote it. What if He neglected his Higher calling and poured His life into His trade. Thank goodness our Lord didn't mistake His trade for His calling.

Another challenging perspective for coaches is to view ourselves as shepherds. Having the heart of a shepherd means that we have the right perspective on the athletes He has entrusted us with. It means that we see our athletes as He sees them. As a college student, I came across a poem that has been etched in my brain all these years. I never really tried to memorize it, but it stuck, and until recently, I didn't know why. I call it "The Shepherd's Poem." It was written by another college student, Bob McNabb, who wanted to make his life count for the sake of the Gospel.

I've just seen the world and I will set it to a rhyme,

the way God sees it all of the time.

It is starving for food in numbers of millions,

while those needing life are counted in billions.

There is a green pasture only a stone's throw away,

but without a Shepherd, in hunger they will stay.

Where are the Shepherds? Where have they gone?

They are all pulling out weeds in their front lawn.

The Shepherds have problems, they will tell you themselves,

the manure from the sheep, oh how it smells.

The Shepherds' problems are important, you see.

What color should the carpet in their clubhouse be?

Nikes or Under Armour, which should the Shepherds wear?

Ask the dying, see if they care.

But I've seen the world the way it can be,

and these things are no longer important to me.

The manure from the sheep certainly does smell,

but what does that matter when sheep go to hell?

Calling all Shepherds, awaken from your sleep.

The Lord is calling, "Feed my sheep."

It's almost as if these are God's words straight from His heart to mine. Could the Lord have chosen this poem to speak to me about where I am right now? Aside from the Bible, this poem captures the heart of God more than anything I have ever read. It challenges me to see my athletes as God sees them—starving for something that only God can give them and only I can feed them. It compels me to be the shepherd mentioned in Jeremiah 3:15: "I will give you shepherds after my own heart, who will lead you with knowledge and wisdom." I can't help but think of athletes who are in need of someone in their lives who will lead them to the green pastures where they can find the unconditional love of the Good Shepherd.

Much like sheep cannot lead themselves to pasture, young people cannot build themselves into responsible adults without leadership, knowledge, and wisdom. They can't teach themselves integrity, discipline, teamwork, and excellence. They need our firm instruction and encouragement. I hope I don't get distracted by the weeds and the manure, and that I can become a man after God's heart who leads with knowledge and wisdom. I am certain that I have not always had this perspective and have squandered many opportunities to feed His sheep. The encouraging news is that shepherding doesn't require great talent or ability, only a willingness to view people the way God views them. Sometimes, this is not easy, but if we look closely, we can see the insecurities of our athletes masked behind their athletic talent. Did you notice the kid who is a follower and will do anything to fit in? What's he searching for? What about the anger and resentment to authority found in some of our athletes? Isn't there something deeper that causes this? Too many times, my response to my athletes' imperfections of character is full of judgment and impatience. I point out their selfish attitude, apathy toward the team, or sense of entitlement, but I never address what they are really seeking. Rather than punish them for their harmful behavior, maybe I should give them direction.

This is not to say that I should ignore things. Correction is necessary sometimes. God uses it. It has been said that the hard correction of God gets our attention, but His love brings us home. Shouldn't that be the goal of a shepherd/coach—to have his sheep return home? Ultimately, we want our athletes to return to the Good Shepherd because they are His, not ours. The Lord is far more concerned about His sheep than He is our programs. This is a humbling truth that we must embrace if we are going to answer the call to feed His sheep.

Whether we see ourselves as more of an ambassador or shepherd, the key is to view yourself as a tool in God's hand. God has given us platforms so we can accomplish His purposes in our lives. A popular song by Chris Tomlin, "Good Good Father," sums up our mission as Christ's ambassadors and shepherds. Two statements in this song capture the Lord's appeal He is making through us: "[He] is a good, good, Father," and "[We] are loved by

Him." When it's all said and done, what do people think of God when they think of me? Can people see a good and loving Heavenly Father who desires a close personal relationship?

Questions for reflection

1. Who has been an ambassador for God in your life?
2. How can we make God relevant to our athlete's lives?
3. How would you summarize our highest calling as a coach?

5
Misplaced Passion

People are going to be passionate about something. Passion is a good thing, but when it is misplaced, it can become destructive. Players, coaches, and fans have all been guilty of worshipping the created and neglecting the creator. It is an easy trap to slip into because of the passion we have for our sports. I have heard it said that football is a great game but it makes a lousy god. The same can be said about any sport or even our hobbies. Maybe that's why the Lord reminds us of this in the very first commandment when He says, "Have no other gods before Me" (Exod. 20:3, NASB).

I find it ironic that the original Olympics were created to honor the gods. Although the Greeks had false gods, at least their original motives were pure. As the games became more important, we find that the Greeks began to lose their focus on the original intent. They started to make idols out of the athletes themselves. Physical fitness and the finely sculpted body became the most admired quality in Greek society. Athletes who brought glory to their city-state by winning events were showered with gifts and privileges and were treated like the gods for whom the games were intended. Doesn't this sound familiar?

It sounds a lot like what we have created in our culture. The original Dream Team from the 1992 Olympic Games is a great example of how we have glamorized and idolized sports and sports figures. The United States had brought together the very best basketball players on the planet; Michael Jordan, Magic Johnson, Larry Bird, David Robinson, Charles Barkley, Karl Malone, John Stockton, Clyde Drexler, Patrick Ewing, and Chris Mullin were part of this star-studded roster. They were remarkable players and an impressive team. They were possibly the most dominant team ever assembled, winning the gold medal and beating their opponents by an average of forty-eight points! Wow! That is impressive. The players on that team were surprised and even uncomfortable with the amount of attention they were getting. Fans and even the athletes they competed against were in awe of them. They would be greeted by large crowds everywhere they went and signed as many autographs for their opponents as they did the fans. In many ways, this dream team mentality has grown since the 1992 Olympics. Athletes and teams can sometimes be idolized much like the Greek athletes of the ancient games.

In the midst of all this hype, we must find the proper perspective. As ambassadors of Christ, our purpose is to bring glory to the Creator, not His creation. We need to recognize God as the Creator and give Him the glory and honor for the things He has created. He is the one who created the things we admire about athletics. The abilities we have, the opportunities we have, and the games themselves ultimately come from God. Even the passion for competition that is so often misplaced comes from God. The competition calls upon our built-in passion and instinct to battle; it brings out the warrior in us all. What a great idea God had when He put that instinct in us. This warrior instinct is responsible for many things good in our world. It is this instinct we must call on many times in our life. Not only has God internally wired us to battle, but He has also gifted us both mentally and physically to compete.

I believe He sits back and enjoys watching what He has created perform. Oh, how He has created some gifted athletes and some gifted minds. I think it gives Him more pleasure than it does us when He sees a game. Much like a proud Father gleaming after His son just scored or did something significant, so is God when His children shine on the fields of play. "That's my boy," may very well be God's heart. Of course, I have no specific biblical reference to back this up, but it is fun to imagine, and I don't think it is too far from the truth. This perspective gives God credit and the glory He deserves.

We know from the scripture that God is a jealous God who doesn't want to share His glory with anyone or anything: "I am the Lord, that is My name; I will not give My glory to another, nor My praise to graven images" (Isa. 42:8, NASB).

It may seem strange to think of God as Jealous. Jealousy from a human perspective usually grows out of insecurity, pride, or covetousness. God's jealousy is not like that. It is not a passing mood with Him. It is the essence of who He is. It is the appropriate expression of His holiness, and it grows from a desire for intimate fellowship with His children. God's jealousy is stirred when His children lose perspective and allow other things to become their god. In Exodus 20, God tells His people to have no other gods before Him or allow any false god rival Him. A few chapters later, the Israelites are found worshipping calves made from gold. How easy it is to allow these rivalries to enter our lives. Players, coaches, and fans all make this mistake. Their passion and commitment to the game they love become a rivalry to God. Their passion is misplaced. God is left out. He is put in a box and basically told He doesn't belong on the field, in the coach's office, or in the locker room. How tragic. Tragic not only because God doesn't receive glory, but also because we miss out on so much that God has to offer if we will just let Him be a part. God is not excluded entirely from this scenario. He is included in pre-game devotions, the reciting of the Lord's Prayer, and of course, the prayers said by both teams and their fans: "Lord, please let us win this game" or "Please, let us make this kick or make this shot." Suddenly, we want to take God out of His box so He can direct the path of the ball as it flies through the air.

It reminds me of the Civil War when both sides invoked God's aid and passionately believed He was on their side. In his Second Inaugural Address, Abraham Lincoln summed up this paradox:

"The prayers of both could not be answered; that of neither has been answered fully. The Almighty has His own purposes."

God is sovereign to determine the outcome of any contest, but that doesn't mean He does. He can't answer the prayers on both sidelines; someone has to be on the losing end. So what does that mean about His involvement with the game? Does he randomly pick and choose which sideline prayers to answer? Does He ignore them all? And most importantly, what are His purposes? Our 16th president had the right perspective on the Civil War. He had big-picture thinking. God's purposes are different than man's. They are much bigger. They are eternal. He is far more interested in what happens *in* us than what happens *to* us, and He will use our victories and defeats to accomplish His work. To God, athletics is a tool, and players and coaches are His workmanship. Our response to this has to be one of coachability. We must be a moldable clay in God's hand. God is trying to finish the work He started in us, but we can't expect God to truly bless our lives if we don't let Him mold us. The encouraging news is that God is committed to finishing the work He started in us. We are a work in progress, and God has a plan for us. God's jealousy is also stirred for His name's sake; or in other words, His reputation: "I shall be jealous for My holy name" (Ezek. 39:25, NASB).

All throughout scripture, God acts or doesn't act on behalf of His name. His desire is for people to know that He is the only true

God that can bring people peace and contentment. In the Old and New Testaments, He goes to great lengths to reveal this truth to man. Today, He uses us to live out this truth and bring Him the glory He deserves.

A very familiar verse in Psalms reminds us that His hand in our life is ultimately for Him: "He guides me in the paths of righteousness for His name's sake" (Ps. 23:3, NASB).

The paths of righteousness He leads us to will bring us peace and protection, but it's for His name's sake, not ours. His reputation is on the line when it comes to the paths we take. In other words, people view God in light of our behavior. Wow, this is an awesome privilege and responsibility. To think that God's reputation is at stake when people look at my coaching is humbling. And people are indeed looking, especially if we claim to be a Christ follower. Woe to me if I misrepresent who God is by not walking the paths of righteousness He has set for me. We must live in such a way as to protect God's reputation, not ours. Far too many times, I have been more concerned about my reputation than God's.

When one of my wrestlers lost his temper and threw his headgear after a loss, I let him have it up one side and down the other. A strong reprimand was definitely in order, but the motives for my words were more about protecting my reputation than God's. I was going to show him and everyone watching that I was a tough coach who didn't tolerate such behavior. These wrong motives led me to behave in such a way that was far from Spirit controlled and far from God-honoring. Later that year, the young man quit the team.

I blew it with him because I was more concerned about my reputation than I was God's. It's not about what people think of me. It's what they think about God when they think about me. God has a path for our career that is a righteous path. It promises to be a path of abundance and prosperity. Not necessarily worldly abundance and prosperity, because God's ultimate goal is not to bring us glory but to bring glory and honor to His name. I pray I will learn to be led into paths of righteousness for "His name's sake." As I look back on my life, I recognize the hand of God working through athletics to accomplish His work in me. I have been a part of winning teams and losing teams. The Lord has used all my experiences to teach me and mold me, and He is still working on me to this day.

We must be careful to keep things in perspective. Sports have been given to us to enjoy, to learn how to be warriors, and to fulfill God's purposes. As a god, it doesn't fill our void. Our void can only be filled through a relationship with Jesus Christ. God offers true and lasting fulfillment, not based on any performance, but solely on His grace.

If you have a relationship with God, don't neglect it. Don't worship what you do and play at worshiping God. Integrate your faith into your career. Don't believe the myth that God doesn't belong on the field, and don't make anything your idol. Use your God-given abilities, passionately follow God's calling on your life, but don't confuse your calling with why you were created. Remember your awesome responsibility to live and coach in such a way that protects the reputation of God.

Questions for reflection

1. How can we use our careers to give God the glory He deserves?
2. How has God used athletics to accomplish His work in your life?
3. How do we protect God's reputation and reveal His true nature as we live our lives before the world?

6
Work as an Offering

I love seeing a room full of athletes working hard. Kids call it "putting in work." I love it even more when the players embrace the grind of hard work because they recognize it helps accomplish team goals. As they sweat and strain, their focus is not on their pain or discomfort, but something bigger. I think there is something in this scene that can teach us about how we view our work.

The Lord revealed this truth to me on a hot late summer afternoon as I walked around my son's recreation league football practice. I was trying to get a little exercise, so instead of just sitting there watching, I decided to put my headphones on and watch as I walked. The Lord chose this odd time to reveal to me an important truth about putting in work. I began to see everything on that field as having the potential to be God-honoring. I don't remember the song I was listening to, but I do remember the sweat, grass stains, drills, hustle from the players, passion from the coaches, and order and organization of the practice. It all fit together in a glorious display of talent and passion.

All too often, I forget that perspective when I get caught up in the particulars of my job. Worship is not limited to singing songs in church. Worship is giving God His worth, which pleases Him. We can make our jobs an offering to the Lord. Work can be worship. I like to remind my athletes that their talent is God-given and that what they do with that talent can bring Him honor. The hard work they put in to develop their talent is a way of saying thank you. The practice time, the mental preparation time, and the off-season training are all part of a process of using what they have been given to ultimately bring honor to God. The Bible calls this a living sacrifice: "Therefore, I urge you brother and sisters, in view of God's mercy, to offer your bodies as a living sacrifice, holy and pleasing to God—this is your true and proper worship" (Rom. 12:1, NIV).

To get a full understanding of this passage, we need to go back a few verses and see what Paul has been talking about. Anytime we see the word *therefore*, we need to ask: what is it there for? In chapter 11, Paul writes a praise to God that ends with these words: "For from him and through him and for him are all things. To him be the glory forever. Amen" (Rom. 11:36, NIV).

That's why we are to offer living sacrifices to God. That's why our talent and time should be an offering that brings pleasure to God. It's because they are from Him, through Him, and for Him. That's the reason for the *therefore*. Can we say that our work is a sacrifice that is holy and pleasing to God?

In the 1924 Olympics, Eric Liddel had decided he would not compete in the 100-meter race because the first heats were always run on Sunday. He chose instead to compete in the 200- and 400-meter events. Most people think of his choice not to run as part of his faith; that is what he is most remembered for. While that is true, I think it was his ambition to win that became a bigger part of his faith. I think he understood what Paul wrote about in Romans 12. Liddel said, "When I run, I feel His pleasure." Running and the way he approached his running became his offering to the Lord. He went on to win the gold in both events, and through this accomplishment, he was able to give the glory to God.

Questions for reflection

1. What does worshipping our work look like? What effects does this wrongly placed worship have on our lives, families, and those we lead?
2. What does worshipping God through our work look like? How does this transform our coaching and those around us?
3. Can you be confident that God is pleased with the work you do? If so, how?

7

Balancing Career and Family

Priorities are determined by how we spend our time and money. The two most revealing things about our priorities are our calendar and our checkbook. For example, I can say that I place a high priority on my marriage, but if I never spend time with my wife, then is it really a priority? The way I spend my time reveals what is important to me. My words about my priorities are empty if they are not backed up by my actions. As coaches, we often speak to our kids about priorities. "Faith, Family, Academics, and Athletics" or "Books, Barbells, and Ball" are often the phrases used to teach our athletes how to prioritize their lives. We do a good job getting this message to our kids, but I am not so sure we aren't just giving this lip service sometimes. It has been said that more is caught than taught, and that is certainly true when it comes to the relationship between players and coaches.

One thing I remember my high school coach saying before a big game is this: "There are only two things more important in our life right now than this upcoming game—your relationship with God and your relationship with your parents." That statement taught me a great deal about priorities. It showed me relationships are the most essential thing in life—my relationship with God and my relationship with my family. Without a sermon outline or Bible verses, my coach gave me a reference point from which to judge the eternal and the temporal. Without realizing it, he laid a foundation that has stuck with me to this day.

His message stuck with me because it wasn't just the words. I caught this message in the way he treated others and the way he valued relationships. Coaches have this kind of influence only when what they do is consistent with what they say. So, do we want our athletes to prioritize Faith and Family first, or are we just saying that? If we put it on a T-shirt or locker room wall, then we need to model it. There is too much at stake not to. Not only are our families at stake, but also the families our athletes will one day lead.

Jesus used a teachable moment to teach this principle to His followers. Mary and Martha were hosting Jesus in their home. While Martha was distracted by her many tasks, her sister, Mary, was sitting at the feet of Jesus, listening to what He said. Martha was upset by the lack of help she was getting from her sister, and she brought her concern to the Lord. Jesus's reply was probably a surprise to Martha. He responded: "Martha, Martha, you are worried and upset about many things, but few things are needed—or indeed only one. Mary has chosen what is better, and it will not be taken away from her" (Luke 10:38-42, NIV).

Jesus was teaching about the priority of relationships. Mary's priorities were right where they needed to be. She was spending quality time with Jesus, not allowing the urgent matters to crowd out the one thing that was necessary. That one necessary thing boils down to relationships, relationships that require distraction-free time.

Distractions to a team and a coach can come in many forms. Voices from the outside, internal strife and conflict, bad calls from officials, and many other things we can't control can quickly take us out of the game mentally. Coaches must be alert to the things that can derail their team and provide redirection and proper focus. This is as important as scouting an opponent and developing a game plan. Distractions can also cause coaches to lose focus, much like they did to Martha. We can become captive to the "tyranny of the urgent." We see so many things that need to be done. After all, Jesus did tell Martha that a "few things are needed." I'm sure that there were things that needed Martha's attention, and to her, they seemed very urgent.

There is a sign that hangs above doorways and in coaches' offices all across this country. It simply says: "Coach your team." The message is to control what you can control and don't allow distractions to steer you from your most important job—coaching your team. The outsider looking in may not understand a sign like this. Isn't that what we should be doing anyway? Why do we need reminders to tell us to do something we should already be doing? It's just not that simple. Unfortunately, some distractions tempt us to make the wrong choice. We need to be like Mary, who chose the right thing, but many times, we end up like Martha. I can identify with Martha. I tend to let my life be ordered by the things that are urgent instead of what is important.

Coaches naturally lean toward Martha-like tendencies. It is part of our DNA, and we try to instill a sense of urgency into our athletes. There are countless demands on our time and attention. This urgency is compounded even more when our very livelihoods depend on whether we win or lose. We are faced with the dilemma that Charles E. Hummel writes about in *Tyranny of the Urgent.* "We have done those things which we ought not to have done, and we have left undone those things which we ought to have done." The question then becomes, how can we achieve balance and make the right choices about how we spend our time? Once again, the Good Coach is our model.

Jesus was a very busy man, but He always made time for the relationships in His life. He frequently broke away from the crowds and spent time with His Heavenly Father. He spent time speaking with the woman at the well. He dedicated countless hours to teaching and training His disciples. He did not finish all the urgent tasks before Him, but He did complete the work which God gave Him to do (John 17:4). He had a sense of a greater purpose and was led by the Spirit. He ordered His life around the things that were eternal, not temporal. He did this by seeking His Father's will in prayer daily. His life was perfectly balanced and directed by His Father's voice, not by urgent demands.

The reality is that a lot of the urgent things we spend our time on are not that important. If we are not careful, we can neglect the important things, like our family relationships. It is the relationships in our lives that will be here long after our seasons and careers are over. Trophies, titles, and rings are treasures that will rust, but unfortunately, families are often sacrificed on the altar of coaching. What does it profit us to build up these earthly treasures and forfeit our families in the process? God's heart breaks for the families that are neglected and torn apart by coaches who give their lives to building a program but have nothing left in their tank for Him or the families He has blessed them with. Spouses and other family members are the ones who make tremendous sacrifices in order for us to do what we love. It has been said that there is a special place in heaven for coaches' wives and I believe it.

I believe the biggest thing coaches can do to show appreciation for those sacrifices is to communicate one thing to our family: "You are more important to me than my job." This has to be more than lip service. This means we have to break away from the urgency of our teams to spend time with our families. How many more films do we have to break down for that to be enough? At some point, we need to stand behind our work. To me, it shows a lack of confidence in your work when you have to break down one more film or stay one more hour just for the sake of saying you worked late. We need to coach and prepare with the conviction that we have done enough to win. We may need to work smarter, but not necessarily harder. Putting your family and marriage on hold until the season is over is harmful. It says, "You are not as important." We would never say that with our actual words, but the sad thing is that it is being said with our actions, with the way we spend our time. Every family is different. I don't know the formula for the balance between your family and career. I can't tell you how much time you need to spend with them. I can only tell you that you must find this balance! There is too much at stake. If we fail at home, we fail! No championship is worth sacrificing our families. I doubt that anyone of us will be sitting in a nursing home saying, "I wish we could have won just one more game." No, the regrets we will have are the broken relationships with our families. If you want to know how you are doing in this area, ask your spouse. Ask them to give you an honest evaluation of the priority you are putting on the family.

I believe it is crucial for us to include our families in our careers as much as possible. There are many supporting roles our family members can participate in. Kids can be ball boys/girls, water boys/girls, and equipment managers and participate in fundraising events. There are many ways our loved ones can get involved. My wife and I have made a tradition of having my athletes over for dinner once a year. This has given my family a chance to get to know the players and feel a connection with them and what I do.

Questions for reflection

1. How can we discern the difference between what is urgent and what is essential?
2. Why is it important to prioritize relationships? Which relationships should be the priority?
3. If more is caught than taught, how can we model proper priorities to our athletes?

Part 2

Leadership Principles from the Master Coach

A familiar cliché in athletics is that it's not where you start, it's where you finish that matters. This is so true. A good coach knows how to finish strong and peak his or her team at the right time. The short ministry of Jesus has many parallels to coaching. His three-year stint with His team was impressive regarding where they started and where they finished. It was indeed a journey with many ups and downs, and if we measured the success of Jesus's early ministry by the performance of His disciples, the results would be erratic at best. Undaunted by the disciples' failures and inconsistencies, however, the Good Coach just coached His team. He led them, transformed them, trained them, and motivated them to impact the world. In doing so, He provided us with principles of leadership that will work for our teams too. This section of the book will take a look at the Good Coach and His methods and will challenge you to steal a page or two from the playbook of Jesus.

8

The Teacher, the Training, and the Task

Follow Me

The calling of the first disciples recorded in the Gospels sounds a lot like a coach recruiting His team. "Follow Me, and I will make you fishers of men" (Matt. 4:19, NASB). In this verse, we see Jesus doing what every coach must learn to do at some level: recruit. In sports, particularly at the college level, recruiting is the lifeline of a program. You are what you recruit. It was a bold statement to ask the disciples to follow Him. Follow a stranger? Why would you do such a thing? They didn't really know Him, yet they wasted no time in leaving everything behind. They certainly did not understand the mission Jesus would be asking of them. Not yet. The Lord did not say, "Follow me, and I will make you successful fishermen (or wealthy men, or even content men)." Jesus sold them on Himself first. The mission would come later. He did not have a polished sales pitch. The disciples had to see something in Christ, something different and something worth following. Christ was fully human and fully God. They didn't know He was God, but they must have seen Godlike qualities in Him. They had to. Why else would they leave their nets and blindly follow a stranger?

These words of Jesus are the words of a coach. The call to "follow me" is what all coaches ask of their athletes. It is a request for the all-important buy-in. Without it, a team will not be successful. The first thing we have to sell our athletes on is us. I'm not talking about a rehearsed three-point speech that impresses people. Those have their place, but it's not speeches and sales pitches that get people to buy in. It is something deeper, something that is sensed more than seen or heard. I believe it was the character of God the disciples sensed on the shores of Galilee. Christ was not an ordinary stranger. There was a safeness in His presence that made them feel as if their leap of faith was not so risky. The character of God dispelled all their fears and allowed them to follow a stranger in an almost reckless fashion.

Coaches would love to have that kind of response to our leadership. I think it is possible if we focus on being more like Christ. It is the character of Christ in us that attracts people to our leadership. No one would ever take a leap of faith into the hands of someone they don't trust, but when people understand how much you love them, they don't have a problem submitting to your authority. I think this was the key to Christ's coaching success.

Like the disciples, our athletes are in some ways taking a leap of faith when they follow our lead. This leap is a whole lot easier if there is safety in doing so and if they have no doubt they are loved just the way they are. If we desire an all-in type mentality, then we have to evaluate our coaching in light of the perceived risk our athletes sense when we ask them to follow us.

Do they sense in us the same things the disciples sensed in Jesus?

Do they know they will be valued unconditionally?

Do they sense Grace?

Do they know we have their best interest at heart?

Do they feel like we are approachable and real?

Oh, how I fall short of these in both my personal life and career! I am selfish. My love can be conditional. At times, I don't treat people with the value they deserve. I can be unapproachable, and I tend to focus on what people deserve rather than being gracious. I can relate to John the Baptist when He said: "He must increase, but I must decrease" (John 3:30, NASB).

I Will Make You

The Lord made it clear that He was going to put His disciples through a training process that would transform their lives. Matthew 4:19 implies a fundamental truth—**disciples are made, not born**. Author Walter Henrichsen wrote a book in 1974 with this same title. The idea behind the book is that people don't come into Christianity equipped to be disciples. They have to be made into a disciple, and they need training and leadership to guide them. Henrichsen emphasizes the role of the leader in equipping and molding men and women to be disciples. This type of transformation requires intentional training. The interaction and words Jesus had with His disciples had a purpose. His intentional leadership had the disciples on a year-round training program, and they didn't even realize it.

Coaching is a lot like disciple-making. Good players are made, not born. Athletes are born, but players have to be made. Player development is crucial to the success of any team. Good coaching is so much more than just throwing athletes out on the field. A team of great athletes with poor coaching and training habits will not reach their potential.

Both athletes and coaches must understand the training that results in true transformation requires two essential things— commitment to change and commitment to a process. This is true in our personal lives too. A willingness to change requires a humility that concedes to the realization that we don't have it all figured out. We have to accept that we are an unfinished work that needs to change into the person God wants us to be.

I am thankful for the truth found in Philippians 1:6, that God is not finished with me yet and that He is committed to completing the work He started in me. Transformation in athletics requires the same humble attitude. Our athletes must buy into the idea of change. All this training and change has to be embraced as a process. Even Jesus operated with this in mind. His work in the lives of His disciples was a process, not an overnight change. Accepting a process becomes an issue of trust, and that is made easier in the context of a loving relationship. If you want your athletes to change and buy in, love them like Jesus does.

Many methods of training work, and a lot of people are willing to claim that their methods are the best. I believe they all work. Simply look around at the different successful programs, and you will find a variety of different training techniques, practice routines, and schemes that work. The common denominators in highly successful programs are principles, not methods. The principles Jesus applied to His team are timeless. They still work. We would be wise to learn these principles and try to apply them to our teams. The next few chapters will take a closer look at some of those principles.

Fishers of Men

The final phase of Jesus's recruitment is the call to the task of being fishers of men. The disciples must have been somewhat confused by this. They were experts at catching fish, not men. I am sure they had questions about what Jesus said. I can see the disciples and Jesus sitting around a campfire and one of them asking: "Uh, Jesus, just what did you mean by fishing for men?"

I think an important principle to understand is that the Lord recruited people to a vision and not a team. The vision Jesus presented struck a nerve with these young fishermen. It was a vision of purpose that involved living for something that had eternal value.

The Lord would have continually had to cast the vision over and over again because the disciples were not exactly quick learners. We see this, as Jesus would perform a miracle or share a parable; then later He would discover that the disciples still did not get it. For coaches, this is a familiar scene. Whether it is the endless repetition of a particular skill or the constant reminders to maintain focus, we can relate to Jesus's attempts to sell His vision. We don't know how long it took, but eventually, the disciples understood what it meant to fish for men, and for the rest of their lives, they lived for that cause.

What would this look like for coaches in today's culture? What is the vision that will attract the kind of people we need on our teams? Like Jesus's call to fish for men, our visions need to have eternal value. We are not, however, going to be successful recruiters if we make our appeal seem religious. Our recruitment platform shouldn't directly be a call to spiritual growth, or to join a church, or give your heart to Jesus. While this is ultimately what we desire for our athletes, we should let the Holy Spirit accomplish these things in our athlete's lives. Our job is to provide the environment where this can happen, then get out of the way and let God do His work. The vision we cast needs to include a purpose that goes beyond winning championships. If you are fortunate enough to be in a successful program, you would be wise to use that success as a recruitment tool. There is indeed nothing wrong with using your past success to lure people to your program, but ultimately, the vision you are recruiting to should be bigger. A vision worth following involves sacrifice and the giving of yourself.

We must sell our athletes on these ideals. One very effective method is to cast the vision for family and brotherhood. We all long for the type of relationships that exist in healthy families. Some of your athletes will cling to this ideal because they have never experienced the true unconditional love that comes with being part of a family. I think you will find that athletes will willingly give of themselves when they understand that their fellow teammate is their brother or sister that is relying on them to do their part. Good coaches understand the power of this principle.

In casting a vision, it is also crucial to communicate the cost involved. In Luke 9:23 (NASB), Jesus says: "If anyone wishes to come after Me, he must deny himself, and take up his cross daily and follow Me." This verse is clear that following Jesus would be no easy task and that it would cost the disciples dearly. The same is true for the athletes we recruit. We need to ensure we are inspiring them with a vision, but also challenging them to count the cost it requires to pursue that vision. We run the risk of recruiting unfaithful followers if we are not clear on the expectations from the outset.

A few of the disciples responded immediately to the Lord's call by dropping their nets or leaving family members behind (Matt. 4:20, Mark 1:20). Others were more cautious and decided on a more gradual approach (John 1:39). Still others turned away, deciding not to follow Jesus's call. It is interesting to me how Jesus changed His approach based on the varied responses to His initial call. When John the Baptist's disciples were following Jesus from a distance, He turned to them and said: "What do you want?" (John 1:38, NIV).

These guys were the cautious followers. They needed more information about this Jesus; they needed more time, and Jesus knew it. So they asked Jesus where He lived. Jesus's words met these guys right where they were at. "Come and see" (John 1:39, NLT). So they went to where Jesus was staying and spent the day with Him. Jesus didn't place an ultimatum on His call. I am so glad when God calls us; He also invites us to come and see. He knows that if we see Him for who He truly is, then we will love and follow Him with reckless abandon just like the disciples eventually did. He is not offended or frustrated by our sometimes overly cautious and delayed response to His call. The invitation to come and see is always open.

Two thousand years later, nothing has changed. People respond to leaders in their own way. Not every athlete is going to drop their nets and immediately buy in to what we say. Some will follow more cautiously, maybe even at a distance at first. And many will never wholly accept or reject our leadership. I have learned that I can't control how someone responds to me, and that worrying about that is inefficient. However, I also can learn a lot from the Good Coach by allowing people to "come and see," and accepting them with patience and grace.

Questions for reflection

1. The Good Coach was able to successfully recruit men and women, convincing them to be all in. What are you trying to get your athletes to buy in to? Is it a vision bigger than a single coach or athlete?
2. What Christ-like qualities do you desire? Why will those qualities attract others to your leadership?
3. Coaches must get their athletes to buy in to a process of training that will make them valuable team members. What about your spiritual training process? What does that process look like? What next step do you need to take?

9
The Unseen

To a culture that loves sports, our job performance is scrutinized and criticized from many different angles. Coach Jesus, like us, had His critics. It seems He spent a lot of time defending His coaching decisions. In Luke 16, we see the Pharisees scoffing at Jesus. Jesus responds: "You are those who justify yourselves in the sight of men, but God knows your hearts; for that which is highly esteemed among men is detestable in the sight of God" (Luke 16:15, NASB).

Jesus gets to the heart of the matter and gives us another vital principle to understand. Kingdom values are very different from worldly values. God looks beyond what men can see. A coach's career is very much in the sight of men and even highly esteemed by some. A lot of things people admire about being a coach are superficial. This is to be understood. It comes with the territory. People want to be associated with winners, and they admire those who consistently win. Winning is an important value to the world, and it better be important to coaches if we are going to survive in this profession. The nature of our job forces us to justify ourselves in the sight of men. If we don't win, our jobs are in jeopardy. Not many people can justify a coach's job if he/she doesn't win.

Ultimately, however, we are not working for men, but for God. God's evaluation is not based on wins. He is concerned with the unseen things of the heart. Our hearts and those of our athletes, not the win-loss column, are His concern.

Sometimes, coaches are admired for their coaching styles. The tough, hardnosed coach seems to be a favorite with many people. There is nothing wrong at all with this coaching style as long as it is genuine and not done to gain the approval of others. We have to be careful not to be like the Pharisees who were more concerned about man's approval than God's. The question for us is, who are we trying to please: men or God? If we seek to please God, then we have to coach within the personalities and gifts He has given us. We can still be passionate, but we can't be posers. The motives of a poser are to gain the attention and approval of men. Personally, I don't want my coaching decisions to be described as *detestable in the sight of God.*

Coaching styles, including wins and losses, aren't the only ways we are judged. At the high school level, we are judged by how many scholarships our kids get offered. Playing at the next level, whatever that level may be, is certainly an admirable goal and something that should be celebrated when our athletes reach that milestone. It is, however, not the goal. It is the icing on the cake. It is something we should help our athletes attain, but by definition, it is a worldly value. This is another value that is *in the sight of men.* I once had a parent of another program tell me their coaches did a poor job of helping their seniors get football scholarships. I personally knew the coaches she was speaking of, and I knew her words stemmed from an uninformed opinion. Her measurement of the program's success was based on a very narrow criterion—how many scholarships were earned.

At the high school level, many parents have missed the point. Earning a college scholarship is not the primary goal of high school sports. There is so much more a kid can gain from participating than gaining a four-year ride. The Kingdom values we offer our athletes can't be measured in dollars and cents or degrees hanging on the wall. What coaches can give lasts a lifetime. What about the values of a strong work ethic, teamwork, and self-sacrifice, just to name a few? These are the values we need to be concerned about as coaches—the unseen matters of the heart.

When Coach Joe Ehrman from Baltimore's Gilman High was asked what kind of team he thought he was going to have, his response was, "I will have to wait and see what kind of husbands and fathers my guys are going to become fifteen years from now." He was operating from a different set of values: Kingdom values. Not only are Kingdom values unseen, but they also take time to mature sometimes. It's part of the law of the harvest. You reap later what you sow. We sow the seeds now, but we must wait patiently like the farmer to see them bear fruit. Hopefully, the young men and women we coach now will be good spouses, parents, and employees one day. We need to wait and see. We can't get sidetracked by the opinions and voices that are making their judgments based purely on worldly values. I wish that more people on the outside of our programs would look beyond the surface and see that we have a lot more to offer our athletes than the superficial worldly values.

Jesus's main critics were the Pharisees, and they were very concerned with outside appearances. We have a lot more to offer our athletes that can be seen on the outside. Criticism from the outside should be put in its proper perspective. Many times, it comes from those who have no clue or have motives other than what is best for our teams. Sometimes, it comes from just plain envy. Maybe, like Jesus reminded the Pharisees, we need to remind our critics that we are operating by a different set of values.

Values are learned. They are not innate. When our athletes come to us, they are already programmed with a certain set of beliefs they learned from their environment. Sometimes, these beliefs are beneficial to our teams, and sometimes, they are harmful. One of our most important unseen tasks is to teach and motivate them to accept the values of the team. Often, this means we have to change their thinking and behaviors. This can be as simple as providing direction that players respond to with ease, or it can be a long process. In Proverbs, children are described as arrows in the quiver of their father. What do arrows need? Direction. Direction to hit the designated target. It is the responsibility of the archer to provide that direction. Our athletes in our quiver are our responsibility. We are the ones that direct them when they are in our control. So the question is, what is the target? Are we teaching them more than just worldly values that men see and admire? Are we directing them to value the things that are unseen, the things God values?

We are certainly not alone when it comes to teaching values to our young men and women. We are partners with parents and other adults who love and care for our kids. My message to parents is that I will help them raise their sons while they are in my hands. I am essentially picking up where the parents left off.

As Bear Bryant once said, "I do my best work with kids who come to me from good Mamas and Daddies." Unfortunately, this is not the case for many of our athletes. Today's society has produced many parents who are simply not doing a good job in raising their children with the right values. In some cases, Mom and Dad have simply chosen to ignore their parental responsibilities. In these situations, we coaches have to roll up our sleeves and do our best to stand in the gap.

There are countless stories of boys who came from horrible situations but were able to look to their coach as a role model and reference point of what it means to be a man. Now, those boys are grown men who are positive leaders in their families and communities and have grown up to understand and appreciate the influence of their coaches in their lives. Then there are the stories of female athletes who grew up in situations where they were devalued, maybe even abused verbally or sexually. In some cases, this type of treatment is part of a terrible cycle that has gone on for generations. But God steps in, and in His sovereignty, places this young lady on the team of a coach who shows the athletes they have beauty and worth because Jesus died for their sins. The coach values them because of who they are, not because of what they can do. Their value is not based on athletic performance and certainly not on what some boyfriend thinks of them. They learn how a lady should be treated. The young athlete grows up and has daughters of her own, and now she will begin a new cycle. The coach has had a powerful impact that will largely go unseen, but it will reap harvests long after the season is over.

Another problem related to focusing on the wrong values is that an ugly sense of entitlement is becoming more prevalent in our society. Many kids enter our programs with the mentality of, "What do you have to offer me?" The parents and athletes are strictly looking at things through the lenses of worldly values. If your program is viewed as unable to provide exposure to bigger and better things, then kids will transfer. I have been on both sides of this as a coach. I have lost athletes due to transfers, and I have received them. I realize that in certain situations, transferring is truly the best thing for the athletes.

My concern is for the integrity of the game, especially at the high school level. Parents and coaches are going to great lengths to make sure these moves don't break the *letter* of the law, but they are violating the *spirit* for which the rules were intended—protecting the integrity of the game. Jesus had a lot to say to those who were overly concerned about the letter of the law while neglecting what is important: "Woe to you scribes and Pharisees, hypocrites! For you tithe mint and dill and cumin, and have neglected the weightier provisions of the law: justice and mercy and faithfulness; but these are the things you should have done without neglecting the others. You blind guides who strain at a gnat and swallow a camel" (Matt. 23:23-24, NASB).

The tithes of mint, dill, and cumin were relatively convenient. The problem the Pharisees had was they were blind to the real demands God required of them: justice, mercy, and faithfulness. There is a lot of gnat-straining going on in high school and college athletics. Governing bodies like the NCAA and high school athletic associations have given coaches rules and regulations to follow. *Most* coaches adhere to these guidelines. Meeting these requirements, however, does not mean we are meeting the demands God requires of us. God calls us to a much higher standard, one that includes weightier provisions: the values of honesty, loyalty, perseverance, unselfishness, and commitment. Aren't these the traits we want our athletes to have? As a parent and a coach, I want my kids to learn the value of something bigger than himself, commitment to something besides himself, and perseverance that requires him to give of himself. What does it teach them when we neglect these values so we can gain an advantage?

Good coaches understand the destruction selfish attitudes have on teams. If left unchecked, the destruction of an all-about-me attitude won't stop with teams. It will also destroy marriages, homes, and relationships for many years down the road. Coaches, it is our job to address this selfish worldly value that has crept into our profession. There is too much at stake not to.

In an effort to gain exposure and earn scholarships, a lot of time and money is being spent on personal trainers, camps, and travel teams. What about the athlete who doesn't have the athletic ability to play at the next level? Is he a failure if he doesn't? These lofty expectations seem to be particularly present at the high school level. I am not discrediting trainers and coaches from the outside. They have their place and can be beneficial. However, they must be honest with the kids and parents about their chances for college scholarships. Many parents and their children have become disillusioned about playing at the next level, and when reality sets in, it is really easy to blame the coach.

The truth is that many high school athletes don't have the physical tools to play in college. That doesn't mean their four years of high school were a waste. The value of their experience goes far beyond a college degree. As a coach, I want my athletes to be focused on having fun, not worrying about whether or not they are performing well enough to get offered by a college. Think about it. Why does a kid come out in the first place? To have fun! We adults have distorted this to the point that it puts undue pressure on our kids and coaches. I am not saying coaches should not work hard to expose our kids to opportunities. That is certainly an aspect of our job we should take seriously, but we must maintain proper perspective when it comes to this issue because so many people have lost sight of what is truly important.

What do we see when we look at our athletes, a star player, or a young man or woman who will one day be a parent? The challenge for us is to teach more than just the skills of the field, but also the skills for life. We need to view our jobs through the lenses of Kingdom values.

Questions for reflection

1. What things do you do as a coach that are often unseen, yet very important?
2. How are God's values and standards different than the world's when it comes to coaching?

3. How can we teach our athletes to focus on what is important and challenge them to a higher standard than the world requires?

10
The 11th-Hour Principle

S ometimes coaching decisions are tough. We can't make everyone happy—Jesus didn't either. The goal is not to make everyone happy; the goal is to treat everyone just as Christ would—with value. That means everyone, even the athlete whose contribution to the team is minimal. I used to work for a coach that offered a challenging perspective. He would say, "Coach them like they are one of your own children." If you have ever had children who are involved in sports, that statement takes on a very personal meaning. You would want your children to get the very best from their coaches. You would expect the coaches' best effort; you would desire the coaches to be competent in what they are doing, and most of all, you would expect them to treat your child with value regardless of his or her ability and contribution to the team. His point was to treat all the players with equal value, coaching everyone the same regardless of their ability. Jesus practiced this same principle in His coaching.

Notice what He teaches in the following parable: "When evening came, the owner of the vineyard said to his foreman, 'Call the laborers and pay them their wages, beginning with the last group to the first.' When those hired about the eleventh hour came, each one received a denarius. When those hired first came, they thought they would receive more; but each of them also received a denarius" (Matt. 20:8-10, NASB).

Wait a minute. That doesn't seem fair. The guys who just showed up got the same amount as the ones who had been there all day? Sounds like bad economics to me. It's not very good for team morale either. The laborers who had been in the heat all day couldn't understand how their contribution wasn't worth more. In their minds and their economy, they should have received more because they contributed more and therefore, deserved more. In God's economy of grace, the word *deserved* does not apply. The heart of God is captured in the landowner's words when he says, "I want to give this last man the same as I gave you" (Matt. 20:14, CSB). God is a giver. He wants to give not based on merit, but based on His amazing grace. This is one of the most powerful truths of the scripture and one of the most important lessons for coaches to apply in their careers. A person's contribution to the team doesn't determine their personal worth and value. The third string tackle has as much value as the star running back. The laborers who showed up at the eleventh hour had as much personal worth as those who bore the heat all day.

Did they contribute as much? Of course not, but that's not how God's economy works. Our culture says differently. We attach multi-million-dollar contracts to star players with great athletic abilities. Production on the fields of play and at the combines determines how much a player is "worth." It is easy for us coaches to follow the trend of our culture and treat our players differently based on their ability, contributions, or potential contributions. We have to be careful here. Our words and decisions as coaches have the power to build up or tear down, and our athletes can quickly see if we are attaching their worth to their performance. We would be wise to practice this 11th-hour principle. This principle eliminates pressure, and it shows our athletes the unconditional love of a Heavenly Father with no strings attached. What an awesome opportunity we have to build up our athletes and give them a healthy sense of self-worth and a proper view of God.

Sadly, I have seen many athletes develop negative self-worth and a shaky foundation that leads to a faulty view of God. Sometimes, well-meaning parents push their kids too much and set a bar of perfection that is impossible to reach. Kids walk away from this experience feeling that there is nothing they can do to please Mom or Dad. They can begin to view God as someone who doesn't accept them for who they are and can never be pleased. To them, God is a demanding authority figure ready to shell out harsh discipline to those who can't measure up. These parents cause damage by putting an enormous amount of pressure on their child. This pressure teaches them that if they perform athletically, then they are lovable, but if they don't perform, then they are not worthy of that love. A child that comes from this type of environment has the odds stacked against them, but a coach can help heal the wounds by demonstrating the unconditional love of Christ.

I witnessed a wrestling match several years ago that involved one of those fathers who just couldn't be pleased. The man's son was a very good wrestler and an impressive physical specimen. He was a lean 215 lbs. and stood about six foot one. We will call him Johnny. It was a match for third place, and Johnny was definitely favored to win. Although Johnny was superior to his opponent, he lacked the confidence to execute his moves. The first two periods were a lot closer than they should have been, and going into the final period, the match was tied. Dad's frustration echoed through the entire gym as he pleaded with his son to "shoot." In wrestling, to shoot means to attack your opponent's legs in an attempt to score a takedown. Johnny gave a half-hearted effort but wasn't able to execute a takedown. Dad's frustration was now spreading to the coach, who soon chimed in with his own negative and sarcastic remarks. This constant barrage of negativity lasted for about two minutes, but I'm sure it seemed longer to Johnny. So much for encouraging words. When Johnny finally decided to shoot, he took his opponent straight to his back and pinned him. Just like that, the match was over impressively. As the official slapped the mat, Johnny immediately rose to his feet with a loud outburst of emotion. But the shout that echoed through the gym that afternoon had an odd, almost disturbing tone. It was not a shout of joy, but more of a release of anger and frustration. The shout was dripping with resentment toward a father who had robbed Johnny of his joy.

A word of caution to parents: don't place such high expectations on your kids that you rob them of the joy they're supposed to experience. When joy is robbed, there is resentment. Joy robbers can come in many forms, including from coaches, but if it comes from parents, the damage can be long-term. No game, no wrestling match or championship is worth that. I don't know where this young man is today or what his relationship with his dad is like. I don't mean to make snap judgments about people based on six minutes of interaction that I witnessed. I could have misread the whole situation, but unfortunately, I don't think I did. I hope that if there were problems, they have been reconciled today.

For most coaches, it is a joy and privilege to coach their own kids. I had that privilege with both of my sons and wouldn't trade it for anything. It allowed us to build some great memories, and it gave me experiences a lot of fathers don't have. This should be a season of joy for you and your child. Can you remember how much you enjoyed watching your kids play on the playground when they were little? Nothing pleases us more than to see our children have fun. Of course, this season comes with potential joy robbers too. The first thief is internal. It is you and me. We can set the bar so high, just like the father in the previous story, that neither you nor your child enjoy the experience. Your expectations may be rooted in motives that are good. You want your daughter to reach her athletic potential. You desire your son to have an opportunity to play at the next level. Nothing wrong with that at all, but be careful that you don't forget about the playground. The experience should be fun for you both. Another thief comes in the form of external pressure. It comes with the territory. Coaches are expected to win, and coaches' kids are expected to be good. It is not that these expectations are too high necessarily, but they are placed on our kids and us by outsiders whose opinions just don't matter. If we are not careful, we can find ourselves trying to please others and live up to their lofty expectations. What happens when you are not winning? What happens when your child is not as good as everyone expects them to be? Can we still find joy? Don't allow your joy to be robbed by the one who comes to "steal, kill, and destroy." This is the time to be a parent first and coach second. As a parent, our role is to protect our family. We are very careful of what we allow to enter our household. We protect the internal from the external. We would fight to the death to keep intruders out of our house. We need to show the same resolve when it comes to keeping our families protected from the external intruders that seek to rob us of our joy.

Early in my career, I was fortunate to have seen wrestling coaches model the right way to coach their sons. From a distance, I was able to see fathers experience the joy of coaching their sons and maintaining a healthy relationship with them. They mentored me without even realizing it by modeling a father's love that wasn't tied to success on the mat. Their relationship with their sons wasn't performance-based. They handled victories and defeats the same way the owner of the vineyard treated the workers of the eleventh hour. I owe a shout-out of gratitude to coaches Weathers, Bailey, and Anderson. Thanks, guys; your example helped both my sons and me enjoy our time together.

Another example of this type of coaching happened on the sidelines of a University of Georgia football game. There was a unique interaction between Mark Richt and his kicker Marshall Morgan. The game was on the line, and just before Morgan was sent to the field for the potential game-winning field goal, Coach Richt told him: "No matter what happens, I still love you." At first, I was puzzled by Coach Richt's words. It seemed like a strange way to take the pressure off his kicker. It appeared that these words were out of place. The reality is that Coach Richt was stealing a page out of Jesus's coaching manual. He was teaching his kicker about the 11th-hour principle—that your value comes from who you are not what you do. By the way, the kick was good, and the Bulldogs won the game.

Questions for reflection

1. The Good Coach taught that everyone has equal value in God's eyes. How can we as coaches practice this principle with our teams?

2. Some of our athletes have built their foundation on the shaky ground of their athletic performance. How can we help them see the danger of this and redirect them to more solid ground?

3. Do you as a coach show that you care for a player even if he or she makes a mistake? How could you do a better job?

11
Principles of Preparation

The hours leading up to a big game can be an emotional roller coaster for both players and coaches. Coaches, like the players, all have their different ways of dealing with this stress. I have seen a coach nervously pace the floor while drinking coffee, and another who was so nervous he couldn't hold down his pre-game meal. I have even heard a story of a coach so overcome with anxiety that he was found lying on the floor in the fetal position. Regardless of their pre-game approach, their hopes will rest on their athletes once the contest starts. The coach will relinquish control and hope that he or she adequately prepared the team. Coaches' work will be put to the test. Their players will undoubtedly face adversity. Will they know how to respond? Will they remain focused? Will they remember what to do in certain situations? Will they remain united and play for a purpose bigger than themselves? All of these questions are magnified in the hours leading up to the contest.

The Good Coach has stood in our shoes. For Jesus and the disciples, the big game would start with Jesus's departure, as He would leave the disciples behind to carry on the Gospel message. The hope of the world rested on eleven men who were about to be thrown into battle. Talk about pressure! In his humanness, the Lord must have had some pre-game jitters. Surely, He could identify with the emotions you and I face as we place our hopes in our players. As the Lord turned over the reins of His ministry, He knew the adversity the disciples would face, but in His deity, He did not worry because He had complete confidence in the way He had empowered and prepared these men. The disciples would overcome adversity and accomplish their mission because they were filled with His Spirit and thoroughly prepared for the challenges that lay ahead of them. A few crucial principles are evident when we look at how the Good Coach prepared his team.

When I have a first-year wrestler on my team, I can't expect him to know what the more experienced guys know. I have to start with the basics—stance, movement, etc. It can be frustrating to coaches and their athletes if our expectations are too high. There was comfort and trust in Jesus's leadership style because He led the disciples from their level of maturity and faithfulness. His expectations were not low; they were personal. He intimately knew the heart of His guys. He knew what they could handle and what they couldn't. He knew them better than they knew themselves, and He tailored the preparation to meet each person right where he was. Like the potter, He already had in mind what He wanted them to become and wasn't distracted by what they had been or what they currently were as He molded them. People are motivated to grow from their level, and it is the leader's job to meet them there.

Meeting us right where we are has always been the way God operates. In Genesis, we see God walking around in the Garden to meet Adam and Eve. Where were they? Hiding because of their sin and shame. I guess you could say it was the first game of hide-and-go-seek and God was "it." But in this game of hide-and-seek, God knew right where they were, and He met them there. There was no place they could hide, and there was no sin that could keep Him from pursuing them. Then there was that night in Bethlehem that God's love reached so far that He became flesh and blood and chose to abide with us. Immanuel, God with us, with us here on the earth that was filled with the same sin and shame that drove Adam and Eve into hiding. Where we reside emotionally or spiritually has never stopped God from meeting us there. Aren't you glad of that?

Patience

The Good Coach understood that even His work was subject to the law of the harvest which says you reap later what you sow. It wasn't until after the resurrection that we see the disciples gaining a full understanding of their mission, and the patient hours of the Lord's coaching bearing fruit. Along the way, there were many ups and downs. Think of all the time He invested into Peter, the man that would deny Him three times. I can imagine Christ pouring His heart out to Thomas so he would have a stronger faith, but he still was labeled a doubter. Then there was that crucial time in Christ's life when He asked some of His disciples to be with Him while He prayed, and they couldn't even stay awake. Time and time again, the disciples seem to miss the point and disappoint. Look at these questions Jesus has for His disciples: "Are you so dull?" (Mark 7:18, NIV). "How long shall I put up with you?" (Mark 9:19, NIV). When it was all said and done, all of the disciples would lose courage and scatter when faced with adversity.

The Lord had plenty of reason to be discouraged and give up on this ragtag group of men, but instead of moaning and groaning like I often do, Jesus often broke away from the crowds and took His concerns about the disciples to His Father. Admittedly, in His humanity, He dealt with the frustrations of coaching and being let down by others. What about you, Coach? Have you been let down by those athletes that you put so much faith in? Maybe it had nothing to do with athletic performance or wins and losses. Perhaps you felt like you went to bat for someone and they didn't appreciate it. Or that you emptied yourself out in hopes that you could change someone, but in the end, they failed you, the team, and themselves. I have been there. People sometimes let you down. They overpromise and under deliver. They never reach their potential. They don't buy into the ideals of team and sacrifice. Coaching athletes like this can test your patience and can cause us to become very negative. You may recognize some of these negative words of which I have been guilty.

- Johnny is too slow.
- Joe is so weak.
- We are terrible.
- We will get our butts kicked if we don't improve.
- Why can't our kids just buy into what we are saying?

Sound familiar? Jesus had plenty of reasons to be negative too, but we don't see Him using negative words. If I were coaching the twelve misfits Jesus had, I think my frustrations would come out in a similar way.

- Peter is so impulsive.
- Thomas's faith is so weak. He doubts everything.
- We can't even drive out demons.
- Satan is going to kick our butts.
- Why can't these guys grasp what I am teaching?

Fortunately, Jesus had much more patience. He most certainly would have talked to God about the disciples, but I am sure His comments were not quite as pessimistic as mine.

Be All There

Early in Jesus's ministry, we read about the disciples, and it is not a very impressive scouting report. It doesn't appear that they are prepared for much of anything. But in the book of Acts, we see an incredible change: "When they saw the courage of Peter and John and realized that they were unschooled, ordinary men, they were astonished and they took note, that these men had been with Jesus" (Acts 4:13, NIV).

Where did this boldness and confidence come from? It came from coaching. You don't go from cowering disciples to courageous followers without some good coaching. Only one thing can explain Peter's and John's transformation—they had "been with Jesus." That's it? The thing that made the biggest transformation for Peter and John was simply being with Jesus. What about the intense evangelistic training and the long hours of memorizing scripture? Surely, it can't be as simple as just being with someone. The concept of *being with* is rooted deeply in the heart of God. Jesus was God's way of being with us. When Jesus returned to the Father, the Holy Spirit was sent to be with us.

As we build our programs and lead our teams, it is vital that we understand the power of just being with someone. Being with someone means you have to be all there. People are motivated when they are given undivided attention. It gives them a sense of self-worth and value. To be all there means you validate someone. The late Pat Summit is a great example of a coach who understood the importance of validating her athletes and giving them a solid foundation. She was once asked about the most important thing she wanted to ingrain in the lives of the women she coached. Besides leaving with a national championship or two, she made sure her athletes were released into the world with confidence. She coached in a way that not only built confident basketball players, but more importantly, also build confident young women who were secure in who they were. Coach Summit found a way to validate her athlete's self-worth without attaching it to basketball.

As a coach, I want my athletes to have that kind of confidence, a confidence grounded in something more solid than football or wrestling. If they depend on their performance to make them feel good about themselves, then I have failed them. I don't want them to feel like they need to have playing time, a winning record, a girlfriend, or a scholarship, or have their name on an honor roll to validate who they are. Ultimately, I want to point them to Jesus, the Good Coach, because He alone can offer them the ultimate victory that leads to confidence and a strong sense of self-worth.

When I look at the way Jesus interacted with people, it is evident that He was all there because people mattered to Him. People got His undivided attention. This is such a challenge for us. It is so much easier to go through the motions and lead without really building relationships or being emotionally invested. I admire coaches who are emotionally invested. Authentic leadership, especially in coaching, must involve our emotions. The time Peter and John spent with their coach was quality and undistracted time. I am sure they felt like they were the only people on earth when they were with Jesus. That type of time was intentional, and it involved the emotions of Jesus, not just His physical presence. Coach Jesus was always all there, and because of that, the disciples were all in.

Family relationships also suffer when we are not all there. There have been many nights I have come home from work, but my mind hasn't. At one point in my career, I actually would bring my work into my bedroom by opening up my computer and logging in to Hudl. My wife would kid me about Hudl being my mistress. There are so many things that distract us from being all there when it comes to leading people relationally. Our families deserve our undistracted time, not the leftovers.

The Lord had an amazing way of preparing people and bringing out their potential. That's how I want to coach. I want to bring out the best in people who, on the surface, don't have a lot to offer. Jesus's coaching record speaks for itself. He looked past all the junk and saw people for what they could become, and in the end, the disciples were equipped and eager to do exactly what they had been trained to do—fish for men. Jesus knows how to prepare people who have junk in their lives. The truth is, we all have junk in our lives, and the athletes we coach bring their junk when they join our programs. I am thankful the Good Coach meets me right where I am, has patience with me, and is all there.

Questions for reflection

1. How can we apply the principle of *meeting people where they are*?

2. Jesus was let down by those He led. What can we learn from Him when this happens in our lives? How should we respond?

3. We want our athletes to be all in. How can we be all there?

12
The Power of a Coach's Words

Words are powerful. They can build up or tear down. Controlling the words that flow from our mouths can be one of the toughest things coaches do. Scripture speaks to this, "But no one can tame the tongue" (James 3:8, NASB). For coaches, our tongue can also be our greatest tool. What a coach says carries more weight than you might think. Our words are noticed and taken to heart.

I remember an incident with my youngest son, Chase, which taught me just how much kids pay attention to what their coach says. I don't recall the specifics of our conversation, but I was trying to correct him on something I had noticed at one of his little league football practices. It was probably something fundamental that I saw wrong with his technique. Now, I'm not that dad that undermines the coach by contradicting him, but I thought I could offer a few pointers that could help my son improve. After all, I had been coaching high school football for over fifteen years. To my dismay, my son really wasn't interested in what I had to say. He kept repeating the words, "My coach says." At first, my pride was hurt. I thought to myself: "I know three times as much football as this rec. league coach." But my years of experience didn't matter. My son was taking to heart what his coach had told him simply because that was his coach. In his young eyes, those words were almost sacred, and for the time being, more important than mine. I realized the best thing for me to do was back off a little bit and not disrupt the respect that his coach had earned.

When coaches earn that kind of respect, their words become powerful tools that not only motivate athletes to improve their athletic performance but also transform their character. It is in this context that we can be intentional with our words. We see Jesus doing this. He recognizes the needs of the people around Him and then intentionally uses words to meet those needs.

One of the most important ways we can encourage our athletes is to affirm them. Words of affirmation are "tell me" words. Young kids will often get straight to the point and pose the question: "Did I do good?" I can picture a smiling young face as he awaits the response to this question. At that moment, he is seeking a declaration that is very important. He is making himself vulnerable, and he is expressing a deep-seated need: affirmation. Essentially, he is saying, "Tell me that I have worth in your eyes." To affirm someone is to validate who they are. It is a stamp of approval on what they have become and are becoming. If we are honest, we all need affirmation deep down inside of us. As we get older, our vocabulary may change, but there is still a childlike question that needs to be answered. "Tell me" is our heart's cry. This is a need that we can't meet ourselves. Positive self-talk simply is not enough. Someone else must see us. Someone else must also assert that, yes, we did well.

One of the most powerful movie scenes I have ever seen is the closing cemetery scene from *Saving Private Ryan*. I tear up every time I see it. Private Ryan, now in his old age, stands at the gravesite of Captain Miller. Miller, played by Tom Hanks, was the man responsible for leading the mission to save Private Ryan. Many men died in that mission. The last words Private Ryan heard from Captain Miller were, "Earn this." Now, decades later, Ryan comes to the grave seeking affirmation. Did he do good? Did he earn it? His family stands close by, which is a testament to the kind of life he lived. But he still has an unmet need. The question is burning inside of him. He has to know. He has to be told. His wife approaches, and he asks her: "Tell me that I was a good man. Tell me that I lived a good life." No one could have affirmed him like his wife, and her response is just what he needed. She simply says, "You are." Her words carried the affirmation he desperately needed. Coaches' words have that same type of power with their athletes. Kids want and need to hear from their coach that they are significant and their efforts are noticed. Our words and our words alone give the stamp of approval for which they are looking.

A word of caution: affirmation and flattery are not the same. Proverbs 28:23 (CSB) gives us some guidelines for knowing the difference. "One who rebukes a person will later find more favor than one who flatters with his tongue." This verse teaches us that there are times when rebuke is needed instead of affirmation, and that flattery gets you nowhere. Sometimes, we just can't affirm certain behaviors, habits, and attitudes. There are times when frank words of truth are what is called for. Jesus spoke these kinds of words plenty of times. Words of truth are as much a part of the process as encouraging words. Sometimes, these words of rebuke sting, but *later*, the person that speaks these words will *find more favor*. This means that one day, the value of our rebuke will be realized and we will find favor in the eyes of the ones we have led. In fact, we will find more favor because the person receiving the rebuke will grow to appreciate it as just what they needed. When the underlying question is, "Am I valued and loved?" the answer must be a clear and resounding YES. But when the question is, "Can I do anything I want?" the answer must be an equally loud and clear NO. No good coach allows a free-for-all type approach when it comes to an off-season program, practices, or implementing a game plan. Our teams provide a unique environment that places much-needed boundaries on our athletes. In addition to this structure and accountability, sometimes our athletes just need an authority figure in their life that has the guts to tell them no. Unfortunately, some of the kids we coach don't hear that word enough, and they struggle submitting to our authority. I do think coaches need to be wise about the things they are saying *no* to. We don't want to be like the religious leaders of Jesus's day who placed heavy burdens on people. I think it is important to pick our battles and create a culture of acceptance and Grace.

Questions for reflection

1. It has been said that life and death are in the power of our words. What are the words of life that we can speak into our athletes/teams?
2. How can we find a balance between harsh truth and flattery?
3. Can you recall words that someone spoke into your life that encouraged and affirmed you? If so, how do those words impact you?

13
Adversity Is an Asset

We all understand the value of putting our athletes through adversity. We have probably learned this principle from our own coaches. We can all tell of stories of brutal conditioning sessions that we suffered through. We probably tell these stories with a bit of pride and compare them to what we make our kids go through. We tell our kids that their conditioning pales in comparison to what we used to do back in the day. The cool thing about this principle is that it didn't originate with our coaches. It started at Galilee Central High School, 31 AD. That's right, Coach Jesus practiced this principle two thousand years ago. Notice how He creates adversity for His team: "Later that night, the boat was in the middle of the lake, and he was alone on land. He saw the disciples straining at the oars, because the wind was against them" (Mark 6:47-48, NIV).

If you have ever been stuck on the water having to paddle against the wind, then you can relate to the disciples' struggle. I have been in this predicament many times, and I can tell you, it is no fun. Jesus had instructed His disciples to go ahead of Him and meet Him in Bethsaida. He knew their trip would be tough. It was designed that way. He could have instructed them to take another route. He could have calmed the wind a lot sooner than He did. Instead, He chose to let them struggle all through the night. It wasn't until shortly before dawn that He walked out on the water, calmed their fears, and made the winds subside. Why did He delay in calming the storm? Could it be that the Lord understood the refining nature of adversity? We become someone that we wouldn't have become if we hadn't gone through the fire. If we persevere, we come out on the other end a changed person.

The experience of adversity makes us who we are. I take issue with the belief that, "Adversity doesn't build character, it reveals it." I have seen this quote on T-shirts and locker room walls, but I don't think that's what the Bible teaches. Specifically, James 1:3-4 seems to teach otherwise. I have to believe that I am an unfinished work. I look at my life and think there is still a lot of work to be done. The adversities I face become the Lord's construction tools. The tombstone of Ruth Graham sums this up nicely. It reads: "End of construction. Thank you for your patience."

The nature of what we do, automatically creates adversity. Whether it's a formidable opponent or tough conditioning session, our athletes will be refined and remade through being a part of our teams. It has been said the greatest reward for our hard work is not what we get from it, but what we become by it. What a privilege we have as coaches to work with young men and women who are becoming something different than they were when they first came to us. I think back to the scene on the boat as Jesus has just calmed the water. What must have been going through His mind? I think He felt a sense of satisfaction because of what His team had just accomplished. There was not a scoreboard on the boat, just some tired disciples who were becoming something different. Something better.

They had just experienced the stiff wind of adversity, and they were well on their way to becoming sold-out followers who would turn the world upside down. Actually, this principle is something Coach Jesus learned from His father. God has always used adversity to accomplish His work and mold His people. Notice what the Lord does with the nation of Israel, and notice why He does it: "These are the nations the Lord left to test all those Israelites who had not experienced any of the wars in Canaan (he did this only to teach warfare to the descendants of the Israelites who had not had previous battle experience): the five rulers of the Philistines, all the Canaanites, the Sidonians, and the Hivites" (Judg. 3:1-3, NIV).

The reason for the adversity was to teach warfare. God could have removed the nations and allowed the Israelites to inherit the land without any opposition. This would have been much easier. After all, the nation had been in bondage and pursued by the mighty Egyptian army and had spent forty years in a desert. You would think they had been through enough stuff that God could have made their lives a little more comfortable. But there was some unfinished business. Although the nation itself had been through a lot, the current generation had some major flaws.

After Joshua's generation died, the next generation "grew up who knew neither the Lord nor what he had done" (Judg. 2:10, NIV). To put this in coaching terms, the nation of Israel was an inexperienced, untested team. Their lack of experience was a glaring weakness. God's solution? Adversity. The nations that would stand in opposition to the Israelites were instruments in God's hand. They would be the adversity God ordained not only to teach His people about Himself, but also how to fight. It makes me wonder, what happened between Joshua's generation and the next? Why didn't this generation know about God like their fathers did? Scripture is not clear, but somewhere along the way, the torch was dropped. It makes me think of parenting and coaching and how vital it is that we pass the torch securely into the next generation's hands. In addition to a relationship with God, the knowledge of warfare must also be passed on to the next generation. Our children, our athletes need to know how to fight. I am not talking about how to shoot a gun or do hand-to-hand combat. Our military leaders do a fantastic job with that. We still need warriors today. We need a younger generation of men and women who will fight for things that are worth fighting for. There is a good fight that Paul talks about in the scripture: "I have fought the good fight, I have finished the race, I have kept the faith" (2 Tim. 4:7, NIV).

The Good Coach

Isn't that what we want from our athletes, for them to fight, finish, and not give up? These are life skills that will take our athletes a lot farther than their athletic ability. I heard Heath Eslinger, the head wrestling Coach at the University of Tennessee, Chattanooga, say that he has kids whose talent can get them onto his wrestling team, but their character will not allow them to stay there. In other words, they don't have the character and mentality to fight, finish, and not give up. Like the Israelites, they don't have the skills of warfare. Somewhere along the way, they didn't learn how to fight. Sure, they are very talented wrestlers, but that only takes them so far. As a high school wrestling coach, I don't take Coach Eslinger's quote lightly. I want to be sure I am doing everything I can to prepare my athletes by developing their character, not just their wrestling skills.

Kids are not going to learn how to be a warrior by playing video games. It takes real-life adversity to develop the skills of a fighter. There is no better place to overcome adversity than the structure of our programs. It's a crucial role we play in passing the torch. Follow the example of the Good Coach and His Father and use adversity as an asset.

Questions for reflection

1. Is there a time in your life that adversity refined you? Explain it.
2. As coaches, how can we use adversity in the lives of our athletes?
3. Can you think of an athlete who went through adversity and came out on the other end a better person? Why did that happen, and what can we learn from them?

14
Winning the Hearts of Your Athletes

G ood leaders are sensitive to the needs of their followers. Being sensitive to a person's needs communicates that their needs are more important to you than what they can do for you. We get a quick glimpse of Jesus doing this in Mark's Gospel: "Then, because so many people were coming and going that they did not even have a chance to eat, he said to them 'Come with me by yourselves to a quiet place and get some rest.' So they went away by themselves in a boat to a solitary place" (Mark 6:31-32, NIV).

So many people were coming and going. Christ's ministry was starting to take off, yet He did not get caught up in the madness. He had the sensitivity to see what was right in front of Him—hungry and tired disciples, and He provided them with just what they needed. His ministry to the masses would have to wait. This simple act must have had a significant impact on the disciples. It must have made them feel as if they were important—that their needs mattered. The Lord was looking out for His guys. He was making a people decision, not a program decision. They would see Jesus not as a taskmaster, but as someone who had their best interest at heart. Eddie Robinson, former Grambling Head Football Coach, once said, "Leadership, like coaching, is fighting for the hearts and souls of men and getting them to believe in you." That's precisely what Jesus was doing here; He was fighting for the disciples' hearts by taking care of their most basic needs. He could have looked right past their needs and continued to minister to all the people who were coming and going, but He chose instead to bestow value on His followers by devoting His time to caring for them. This is the core of leadership: winning the hearts of your followers. Jesus and Coach Robinson both understood this critical principle. We would all be wise to apply this principle to our coaching.

I have to ask myself, "Do I see the needs of my athletes who are right in front of me? Do I have the discernment and sensitivity to lead with compassion, or am I too concerned with the big picture?" This one hurts. If I'm honest, my attitude toward my athletes is anything but compassionate. Many times, I don't notice the unspoken and unseen needs because I'm too busy or too concerned about all the other things that come with my job.

Let's look at a hypothetical situation where this principle could be applied. A new coach comes to town and takes over a program that has had three different head coaches in the last five years. The players on the team, especially the seniors, are frustrated, but they're willing to see what this new coach has to offer. The new coach meets the players and quickly begins making the changes he thinks are needed. Things have been lax with the previous staffs, to say the least. There has been a lack of accountability and discipline, and the overall expectations are meager—and last year's 2–8 record shows it. As new changes are put into place, several of the seniors are beginning to resist the new expectations passively and are not indicating the type of leadership the coach needs. From here, there are two ways this scenario could play out.

Option #1: The coaching staff meets, discusses the problems, and settles on the most logical and easiest thing to do—focus on the younger kids and start building for the future. It's just not worth it to focus on the seniors. They are too far gone and entrenched in bad habits that there is no way you can get through to them. Besides, your younger classes are talented, and if you can get through to them, you have a chance to be pretty good next year and the year after. The staff's focus on the underclassmen comes at the expense of the seniors. They get less attention from the coaches and fewer reps at practice. Some of them lose their starting jobs to younger players with more potential. The passive resistance of the seniors begins to escalate to more aggressive acts of mutiny. So, as the season drudges along, frustrations will run high, and some of the upperclassmen will decide to quit. This, of course, does not bother the coaching staff at all. They are glad to see some of them go. The season continues with constant resistance to the new coaching changes. Both players and coaches reach a point of apathy, and everyone is glad to see the season come to an end.

Okay, at the risk of sounding cliché, I am going to go ahead and pose the question, what would Jesus do? But isn't that what a Christian coach should ask? I mean, this scenario is a widespread occurrence. If you coach for any length of time, you have either lived this or you will. To know what Jesus would do, we must realize that everything He did on earth was in the context of a loving relationship. When Jesus said, "Come with me by yourselves to a quiet place and get some rest," His motivation was love. In meeting the disciples' most basic need, He was communicating their value and worth. It's interesting that we don't see the disciples saying that they were hungry and tired. They did not tell Jesus their needs, but He knew them anyway. Now, what about those seniors on the team? What are their needs that they are not telling you? Like the disciples, their needs are real and right in front of us. Can we see it? What is their resistance saying? The choice boils down to the same selection Jesus made. He chose to meet the needs of the people right in front of Him rather than focus on His ministry. He made a people decision, not a program decision.

So, how about another approach to our scenario that has a much better ending?

Option #2: The coaching staff meets, discusses the problems, and decides to work hard at building relationships with those seniors. They invite them over to their house and enjoy getting to know them.

They ask them questions and learn about their family situation. Slowly, within the context of a player-coach relationship, unspoken needs are beginning to be met. Discipline is still enforced, and the players are still held to a high standard. It takes time and there is still occasional resistance, but over time, walls begin to come down. Trust is earned. Then the players start to see that their coaches care about them. Their worth and value are affirmed. The team goes on to finish with an 8–3 record, reestablishing the program as a state power. Both coaches and players walk away with a sense of accomplishment. More importantly, the coaching staff has won the team's heart and provided a handful of young athletes just what they needed—accountability, discipline, and affirmation through a relationship.

Questions for reflection

1. What are the deeper needs of our athletes? How can we recognize these needs?
2. Jesus made people decisions, not program decisions. How can we do this and still build strong programs?
3. In the busyness of life, what are some things we could implement to encourage our athletes on a daily basis?

15
Team Unity

Team unity is crucial to the success of our team, and a great deal of scripture is devoted to this topic. Your athletes can buy into you and your vision, but if there is division among them, your season is destined for failure and frustration. The best teams are the ones who are unified in their pursuit of the team's goals. You don't have to be a coach to recognize the power of unity working in teams. Even casual sports fans can recognize when a less talented team wins a game or championships because they bought into the idea of playing as one. When we peel back the layers of unity in scripture, we see that there is a deeper value found in this principle. It is more than just winning games; it is about making a statement. Scripture makes it clear that unity makes a statement to the world. Jesus prayed for unity among believers for their own good but also for the sake of the world. In the words of Jesus, notice the potential influence unity can have on the world: "So that they may be brought to complete unity. Then the world will know that you sent me and have loved them even as you have loved me" (John 17:23, NIV).

We see two desires of God's heart in this verse. He desires unity among His children, and He wants the world to know who He is. In two thousand years, nothing has changed. God still desires these things for us and the lost world. This portion of Jesus's prayer was not for the twelve disciples; it was for "those who will believe in me through their message" (John 17:20, NIV)—that's you and me. We can make a statement by living in unity with each other and by promoting it on our teams. We can have a powerful testimony in a culture that sees so much division.

I believe our teams can point people to God and provide hope specifically in the area of racial unity. No other institution in our culture can bring people together more than sports. It has always been that way. Racial barriers have been broken time and time again on teams across our country. Hollywood has made fortunes by putting these stories on screen. These great movies have been so successful because they strike a nerve. There is something about unity and reconciliation that is powerful. Deep down, we desire it because God wants it. I would argue that there are countless lesser-known stories of racial reconciliation and progress that can be found on the teams across our country over the last several decades, even in the lives of your coaches. The stories may not have received as much attention as Jackie Robinson's, but they are no less important and can make a powerful statement about the power of God to bring people together. With the number of kids participating in organized sports at an all-time high, coaches have a larger platform than ever to model and teach unity between the races. Maybe the scripts of our stories don't end with a state championship like in *Remember the*

Titans. Maybe it is as simple as attitudes being changed. Perhaps through our modeling and teaching, our athletes will begin to question the lies they have bought into. Many of these lies have been sold to them by an older generation of people living with the fear of the unknown, resentment, and unhealed wounds of the past. What if our programs became the learning grounds for a new generation that enters adulthood armed with the truth and a desire for complete racial unity. Now that is making a statement.

Jesus has stood in our shoes and understands the challenges that come with building unity. He assembled a team of men who were subject to the same temptations of division and discord that plague our teams today. Building and maintaining unity is a huge challenge for any coach, and we would be wise to look closely at how Coach Jesus approached this issue.

Let me provide a little backdrop. Jesus's ministry is well underway. News about Him has widely spread that He has increased His followers. In addition to the twelve disciples, many others are now following Jesus. Seventy others have been sent out ahead of Jesus, and now, they have just returned with good reports about their journey. Jesus listens to their reports and shares some words of encouragement for them: "Then turning to his disciples, He said privately, 'The eyes that see the things you see are blessed! For I tell you that many prophets and kings wanted to see the things you see yet didn't see them; to hear the things you hear yet didn't hear them'" (Luke 10:23-24, CSB).

There is one word in this passage that I think has a tremendous impact on team unity—privately. Jesus chose to turn away from the larger crowd and communicate a message for no one else except His disciples. This message found in His words is undoubtedly important, but the private nature of Jesus's words helped build a sense of unity, closeness, exclusiveness, and pride. The twelve were the inner circle of Jesus's ministry, and I believe the Lord was instilling into them a sense of pride about whom they were. For teams to unify completely, they must have an inner-circle mentality. I am not referring to an *us against the world* approach, but more of a culture of intimacy that can only exist between people who are on the inside. The people on the inside share common experiences. Jesus described these experiences as what the eyes see and the ears hear. He went on to say that it is through these experiences that the disciples were blessed. The blessing was in the experience, and the experience was reserved for His team of twelve. I can see the disciples' chests swelling with pride. "We have seen and heard things that kings and prophets long for. We are special."

The Lord had His share of challenges in regard to building team unity. The biggest challenge He faced is the same one we face today—selfishness. It is a part of our nature as sinful men and women, and it is magnified by a culture that teaches "it's all about me." In the Gospel of Mark, we see selfishness rearing its ugly head and threatening to divide the disciples. It came in the form of a request from James and John: "Let one of us sit at your right hand the other on your left in your glory" (Mark 10:37, NIV).

Really? Two of the best players on Christ's team said this? You would expect this from Judas or maybe another lesser-known disciple, but not these two guys. James and John were two of the stars on Christ's team who would've been chosen as team captains. It humors me to imagine James and John as they sat around and discussed how they would present this question to Jesus. I mean, this apparently wasn't a spontaneous question. They put some thought and planning into this.

I wonder if they rehearsed with each other how they would pose the question. Maybe they drew straws to see who would do the speaking. Their request reveals their desire for glory. They wanted a part of Christ's glory. So, as tends to happen, word of this request spread to the other disciples, and the scripture says they were offended by James and John. It was a 10 to 2 split. The actions and words of the two threatened to divide the team. Sound familiar, Coach? Have you ever had a threat to your team unity because of careless words that were spoken, posted, or tweeted? Maybe you have had some bad apples that threaten to destroy your team. They must be dealt with. Jesus responded with, "You don't know what you are asking" (Matt. 20:22, NIV), and of course, they didn't. They were as clueless as our athletes sometimes are today. I feel like I would have given James and John a butt chewing at this point. How could they have the nerve to think this was all about them? Jesus's response was much calmer and effective. Knowing the feelings of the other ten, the Lord called the disciples together for another private conversation.

It's important to point out that Jesus didn't sweep this issue under the rug. He addressed it directly. Even though the selfishness of just two disciples caused the problem, it was an inner circle issue that needed to be addressed with the entire team. Jesus used this opportunity as a teachable moment and made sure all twelve disciples heard the message loud and clear. His words hit home to the disciple just as they do to you and me today: "Whoever wants to become great among you must be your servant, and whoever wants to be first must be a slave of all. For even the son of man did not come to be served, but to serve, and to give his life as a ransom for many" (Mark 10:43-45, NIV).

The solution to selfishness is to think counter-culturally to what we hear today. It is the only solution. Those wanting to be first must be willing to take on an unselfish role of a servant. This applies to coaches and players. It involves giving up personal rights you think you may have and being willing to live a life of giving, not receiving. What a challenge we have to lead in this way. Even more so is the challenge to lead others down this path that goes against everything the world is telling them.

Servant leadership produces fruit that is largely unseen by the world. Actually, most of the things mentioned in this book will go unnoticed by the world. That's okay because God sees it. God sees everything about you, your team, and your job from a perspective that is perfect. His viewpoint looks deep into your heart and the hearts of your athletes. I am so humbled that He chooses me to impact the lives of young men and that He provides me with proven coaching methods to accomplish His work.

Reverend Billy Graham once said: "A coach will impact more people in one year than the average person will an entire lifetime." If I believe this, then I have to understand the awesome responsibility the Lord gives me. I believe that there are a handful of experiences early in a person's life that defines who they will become. I don't know about you, but that gives me a sense of urgency to get it right. Can my athletes say that they are blessed by the experience of being on my team? Do the things their eyes see and ears hear give them an experience that blesses their lives and sets them on a course for real success—a relationship with Jesus? There is too much at stake not to lean in and listen closely to God's voice. As we begin to gain His perspective, we can see that the best thing we can do for our athletes and ourselves is to follow in the footsteps of the Good Coach.

Questions for reflection

1. Why does God devote so much attention to the topic of unity? Why should coaches do the same with their teams?
2. The Good Coach had two of His best players cause division among His team. What can we learn from Him about dealing with selfish attitudes?
3. What things have you done as a coach to promote unity on your team?

Final Thoughts

The perspective and principles that have been shared in this book all point to a loving Father. Our loving Father wants the same things for us that Jesus wanted for His disciples. He wants to win our hearts. Has He won yours? You can probably think of athletes you have coached that are just not quite sure whether to trust you and buy into what you are saying. Is that you in your faith journey? If the answer is yes, then that's okay because God will meet you right where you are. He is not offended or annoyed by your lack of faith. He is patient, and when we're not all in, He is all there.

If coaching is taking athletes somewhere they can't go by themselves, then that is just what God wants to do in your life. He longs to bring you into a relationship with Him that is real, relevant, and life-changing. That relationship journey begins at the cross. That's where the Good Coach's journey took Him. After living in our shoes, being tempted in every way yet without sin, He laid down His whistle and hung on a cross. Now, He sits at the right hand of the Father. He sits there with a heart of empathy because He knows exactly how you feel. For coaches, He is our guide that has been there and done that. Now, He wants to meet you wherever you are along your journey and coach you to a place you can't go on your own. Be coachable. Accept His invitation. Follow in the footsteps of the Good Coach.